THE BIGS

Ben Carpenter

The Bigs

The Secrets Nobody Tells Students and Young Professionals About How to:

- CHOOSE A CAREER
- FIND A GREAT JOB
- DO A GREAT JOB
- BE A LEADER
- START A BUSINESS
- MANAGE YOUR MONEY
- STAY OUT OF TROUBLE
- LIVE A HAPPY LIFE

WILEY

For general information about our other products and services, please contact our Customer Care Department within the United States at (800) 762-2974, outside the United States at (317) 572-3993 or fax (317) 572-4002.

Wiley publishes in a variety of print and electronic formats and by print-on-demand. Some material included with standard print versions of this book may not be included in e-books or in print-on-demand. If this book refers to media such as a CD or DVD that is not included in the version you purchased, you may download this material at http://booksupport.wiley.com. For more information about Wiley products, visit www.wiley.com.

ISBN 978-1-118-91702-2; (cloth) ISBN 978-1-118-91871-5 (ebk);
ISBN 978-1-118-91872-2 (ebk)

Printed in the United States of America

10 9 8 7 6 5 4 3 2

Contents

Nothing in the world is worth having or worth doing unless it means effort, pain, difficulty.... I have never in my life envied a human being who led an easy life. I have envied a great many people who led difficult lives and led them well.

—Theodore Roosevelt

Preface

Welcome to the Big Leagues

When you become responsible for yourself, and you are being paid to do a job, you are in the big leagues. The real world is tough, and competitive, and a lot is expected of you. As *The New Yorker* cartoon spoofs, no one will be handing you a bouquet of flowers.

"Welcome to the big leagues."
The New Yorker, August 13 and 20, 2012

In baseball, "the bigs" is slang for the big leagues and the expression "Welcome to the big leagues" refers to the specific act of a veteran pitcher (identified in the cartoon by the stubble on his face) throwing a fastball, which often exceeds 90 mph, at a rookie batter from the opposing team the first time they face each other. The purpose of this violent and potentially dangerous act is to attempt to intimidate the rookie to see if he is tough enough to play with the big boys in the big leagues.

HOW *THE BIGS* CAME TO BE

This genesis of this book, however, wasn't a fastball. It was a curveball thrown at me by my eldest daughter, Avery. After a year-long search, she received her first post-college job offer. The job was to be the assistant to the co-executive producer of a new network daytime TV talk show. The co-executive producer, Kathy, called Avery personally and asked her to start *this* Monday—just four days away.

When Avery told me the good news I was ecstatic. This was Avery's dream job and I knew she would be terrific at it. I was over the moon with excitement and happiness for her. That is…until the next day when Avery threw me the curveball in the form of an email to her mother, Leigh, and me. The email was titled, "Is This Okay to Send?" Addressed to her new boss it read:

Hi Kathy,

I can start whenever you need me to but, if possible, I would like to start a week from Monday because that would allow me to tie up some loose ends. I am looking forward to working with you.

Best,

Avery

"LOOSE ENDS?!…A WEEK FROM MONDAY?!" As I read that sentence over and over, I could feel my eyes bugging out and my blood pressure rising. I wasn't mad at Avery; I was scared for her. I fully understood what was behind Avery's desire to start a week later—she wanted to go apartment hunting. Avery had two college girlfriends lined up to live with, but she hadn't been able to get an apartment until she got a job, and Avery couldn't wait to leave home and move into the city.

While I sympathized with Avery's desire to move, when I read her email the first thought that entered my mind was my daughter had just been offered a job in the *big leagues* and she had *no idea* what was expected. To me, this was as if Avery had just been given the opportunity to play center field for the New York Yankees and she wanted to ask the team's general manager if she could report a week late! At that moment I realized, despite being a 23-year-old college graduate with an immense amount of intelligence and charm, Avery had a great deal to learn about the working world. As you know, fear is a great motivator. Immediately, after responding to Avery and telling her *not* to send the email, in a full-blown panic, I sat down and wrote a stream of consciousness email with bullet points for her to follow in her new job.

A few hours later, I emailed my list to Avery as well as to my long-time administrative assistant and friend, Lori Beaton. Lori quickly responded saying she had some additional thoughts for Avery and I should "write a book" on the topic. I never considered writing a book, but I had intended to jot down a list of life advice for my three daughters. After a series of health scares, I feel my mortality much more than a normal 55-year-old. In my role as my daughters protector, I wanted to be certain they could benefit from my experience, knowledge and mistakes even if I wasn't there to tell them.

So here I am…it's 2:30 a.m. Sunday morning and Avery is just getting in from a night out partying (better now than after she starts her job on Monday)…. I am unable to sleep…sitting in the kitchen…writing these thoughts down….Leigh, on her way to bed alone for the third night in a row, expressed her amazement (annoyance?) that I have become obsessed with writing this book when…just a few days ago…I hadn't ever mentioned writing a book…. She has a point…all I know is Avery getting her first job has energized and scared me, and I won't be able to sleep until I have gotten these thoughts out of my head and onto this paper….

Introduction

Before *The Bigs*

The Bigs is unique. It is not a memoir. It is not a how-to book. It is not a self-help book, and it is not a collection of entertaining war stories from the front lines of commerce. Instead, it's all of these. Also, it's all true. The stories happened just as described and the advice is hard-earned knowledge from what I've done right, done wrong, and seen others do likewise. *The Bigs* is also unique in its organization and style. Part One, "How to Survive, Thrive, and Have Fun in the Big Leagues," is written in the form of a liberal arts education—it teaches you how to think about the kinds of issues you will encounter in the real world. Part Two, "How to Choose, Get, and Do a Great Job," is written in the form of a graduate school education—it teaches you specifically how to accomplish these critically important tasks.

The Bigs is also a wild ride, which includes me trying to climb the corporate ladder while simultaneously owning and managing an out-of-control bar in Manhattan, slipping badly and almost falling off the ladder, coming perilously close to dying, and finally helping build and becoming the Co-CEO of a remarkably successful major international investment company. However, we start with this Introduction which tells the story, in brief, of my childhood/teen experiences and the impact they had on my psychological make-up. It is important for you to understand who a person really is before you trust the advice they give. After this Introduction, I feel reasonably comfortable I will pass your honesty test. However, you may well decide some of my judgment was questionable (to say the least). Well…since I'm unwilling to rewrite history…let me just tell you what happened.…

JUNIOR HIGH SCHOOL

In the spring of my seventh grade my family moved from Missouri to Williamstown, Massachusetts (a bucolic town in the northwest corner of Massachusetts). This was the fourth town, in the fourth state, I had lived in during the previous four years.

The Flagpole

My new school was Mount Greylock Regional High which included grades 7-12 under one roof. Despite being set on a hill with a gorgeous panoramic view of its namesake, Mount Greylock had its fair share of issues. Not only was there a huge age spread among the students, there was also a huge socioeconomic chasm. This was because the school served Williamstown (with its sons and daughters of the Williams College faculty) as well as Lanesboro (an old iron ore mining town whose glory days were long gone). It must have been something in the water, because there was a marked difference in the physical profile of the boys from the two towns. In each grade, while roughly the same height, Lanesboro boys were generally 50 percent heavier with 200 percent more facial and body hair. The result was the Lanesboro guys looked five years older and in my seventh grade class it appeared as if half the boys should be seniors preparing to graduate.

The early 70s were well before small backpacks became standard issue for students and the Williamstown kids would walk around between classes with huge stacks of notebooks and textbooks under their arms. At the opposite end of the spectrum were the older Lanesboro "students" who were way too cool for school (and even too cool to play organized sports). Their main interests were cigarettes, motorcycles, and girls. I quickly learned the one school sport Lanesboro guys *did* enjoy was prowling the halls looking for unsuspecting small Williamstown boys whose books they would knock to the floor and laugh like hyenas as their victims scrambled to pick up their papers and dignity. This was such a popular pastime with the Lanesboro crowd it was common to see Williamstown junior high boys scurrying about between classes clutching their books with two hands like skinny miniature NFL running backs protecting the football. Mount Greylock may have been one school, however, it was really two separate worlds.

Being a seventh grade new kid from Williamstown, and looking like the completed figure in a game of Hangman, I was a perfect target for the hyenas. After being at Mount Greylock less than a month, late one afternoon a pack of badass Lanesboro guys, looking more like Hells Angels than high school students, grabbed me in the main hallway. I knew I was in trouble when they lifted me up and carried me, kicking and squirming wildly, out the front doors straight ahead to the enormous flagpole in the middle of a large lawn. The flagpole was encircled by 25 school buses, parked bumper-to-bumper, ready to take everyone home. The effect created by these school buses, packed tightly in an elliptical formation, was that of a bright yellow Roman amphitheater.

Despite my frantic efforts to fight back, my pants were pulled down to my ankles, I was hoisted up a few feet, and the back of my tighty whities were impaled on the flagpole cleat—giving me a wedgie of historic proportions. As the Lanesboro guys walked away laughing and slapping each other on the back, they left me attached to The Flagpole. I was three feet off the ground, my naked legs bound together by my pants, and my arms flailing around like some deranged scarecrow attempting to fly. Since I wasn't trying to draw attention to my predicament (good luck with that), all this frantic movement must have looked like a silent movie with the projector sped up.

Then I heard something truly terrifying—the end of school bell screaming like a Hitchcock murder victim. I knew, in just a few moments, my humiliation would be going viral the old fashioned way. As I was preparing myself for a life of perpetual ridicule, suddenly, the back of my underwear ripped apart and I awkwardly fell to the ground. Adding injury to insult, my head snapped back and slammed into the base of the metal flagpole with a loud *PING* which reverberated inside and outside my skull. I got to my feet, pulled up my pants, and slowly began moving in the direction of my bus—feeling like a punch drunk fighter and walking with the painful gait of an old bowlegged cowboy. Simultaneously, the front doors of the school burst open with 600 students now joyously free, but mercifully oblivious to the priceless spectacle which had just eluded them.

I wasn't quite so lucky with my bus driver whom thereafter, whenever I got on his bus, gave me a compassionate smile and slight nod. With no words spoken we would both, for an instant, flashback to that day and my extraordinary encounter with The Flagpole. Interestingly, during my four and a half years at Mount Greylock, as far as I know, I was the only one subjected to a flagpole "hanging." Why that is I have no idea, but that oddity did make me even more grateful for my narrow escape.

It would be satisfying to tell you I exacted my revenge on the Lanesboro guys in some bold, brave and creative way, however, what actually happened is they became my friends. The reason was ice hockey. The following year, as an eighth grader, I was one of the better players on the high school varsity. Ice hockey, because of its inherent violence and glorification of fighting, was the one school sanctioned sport Lanesboro guys participated in and/or respected.

Our shared interest in ice hockey, disinterest in academics and generally rebellious attitude towards authority became the basis for many of my high school friendships.

THE NEW KID

While my introduction to The Flagpole had taken me by surprise, I can't say I was shocked. That's because, over the past four years, I had gotten used to being surprised. When I was nine years old my world turned upside down. Until then things had been pretty darn good. I was the second oldest of five children and grew up in Lake Forest, Illinois—a beautiful suburb of Chicago. As a boy I spent weekends with my extended family on both sides, passed sunshine-filled summers going to camp, and loved playing baseball, ice hockey and riding my bike around the neighborhood to visit friends I had known my entire life. Little did I know storm clouds were rolling in and my family was in for some heavy weather.

The first bolt of lightning shattered my reality—we were moving! I was in fourth grade when my father lost his job at the bank. Using his engineering degree from Northwestern, he found a job in Peterborough, New Hampshire running a small manufacturing plant. I remember my first night in the new town lying in bed, sobbing uncontrollably, while my mother sat beside me and said it would all be okay. I couldn't believe what had happened. That move set the pattern for the next six years; every second year my father lost his job and our family of seven was forced to pack up and move. I spent fourth and fifth grades in New Hampshire, sixth and seventh grades in Missouri, before moving to Massachusetts for my eighth through eleventh grade years. Over a period of 10 years, I attended six different schools in five different states.

While difficult, moving during those formative years did teach me how to make new friends. Sports helped a great deal because, while I was not some remarkable athlete, I was always good enough to make the team and be a significant contributor. Since all these moves were the result of my father being unable to keep a job, our family's financial situation steadily deteriorated and a disquieting sense of financial insecurity was ever-present.

HIGH SCHOOL

It would be convenient to blame all my troubles in high school on my friends from Lanesboro, but I know I have to take the lion's share of responsibility for my behavior.

The Bug

In Williamstown, my family had two cars: a station wagon for Mom and a VW Bug for Dad. Not surprisingly, I wasn't allowed near the more valuable station wagon so my ride was The Bug. There was only one problem with The Bug—it had those huge rounded fenders that stuck out and, when I was out drinking with my buddies, we always seemed to have terrible luck with them.

Time and again, I would bring The Bug home with a large new dent in one of the fenders. Since money was tight, my father's answer was to ignore the damage and his Bug soon began to look like a veteran of the demolition derby circuit. One of the Bug's four fenders apparently lived a charmed life and, despite the bad luck which was regularly visited upon his brethren, he remained unscathed—until one night when the odds finally caught up with him.

I drove home in the wee hours and passed out on my bed. The next thing I knew it was morning and I was being dragged out of bed, by my legs, by my normally mild-mannered father. I scrambled to my feet and Dad, with no experience beating his children, stood there trembling with anger. Finally, he shook his head like a bull about to charge. My father, however, was no animal and instead of charging he started kicking my shins wildly while sputtering and explaining between labored breaths, "*I didn't say anything about the first fender…the second fender…or the third fender…but you have now ruined all four of them…God Damn It!*"

After the last kick, Dad staggered back two steps and I could see in his eyes his anger was spent. He seemed surprised and embarrassed by what just transpired and he mumbled, "*Okay then*" and walked out of my room. While Dad was embarrassed, I was ashamed I upset him to that extent. That was the last time Dad and his Bug had to pay the price for my reckless nights out.

A Full Moon

Though I didn't care much for school, I did love sports and that is where I channeled my competitive spirit. My junior year I was elected co-captain of the varsity ice hockey team. All was good until on our way home from our last regular season game, to celebrate a surprisingly successful season, I decided it would be a good idea to "hang a moon" out the window of the bus. My coach, who ran the woodworking shop at school, decided this was a major transgression and he kicked me off the team. Not satisfied with punishing just me, the coach used this incident as the reason to withdraw Mount Greylock from the Western Massachusetts State Tournament our team had qualified for. (As far as I knew, this was the first time the Mounties had *ever* qualified for the state tournament.) This seemed to me, both then and now, a ludicrous overreaction to a patently victimless crime, but it nevertheless was a source of considerable angst and embarrassment for me. However, this incident was not enough to deter me from continuing to hurtle down the path I was on.

Those Two Words

The next highlight of my high school experience occurred just a few months later during baseball season. I was the starting center fielder on the varsity. One day at practice, as I was walking out to my position, I heard the coach yell, "*Carpenter—hustle out there!*" I don't remember what went through my mind at that instant, but I do remember what I did—which was whirl around and yell back at the coach, "*Fuck You!*" Well that did it…kicked off my second team in two seasons.

I still don't know why I felt compelled to swear at my coach. All he had done was to say something baseball coaches, from Little League on, say almost every day at practice. I guess the best explanation is that it was simply a continuation of my irresponsible, and at times unexplainable, behavior during that stage in my life. What I know for certain is there was one person who, seeing the firestorm I had ignited, rushed into the burning building to save me.

GOING AWAY

Somehow, my mother convinced the highly regarded Hotchkiss School to accept me. I think a big factor was that in the early 1970s boarding schools were going through some relatively lean times. However, due to my barely mediocre transcript, I would have to repeat junior year. I also don't know how my parents scraped together the tuition money, but somehow they managed.

From the moment I stepped foot on campus, I loved it. The school was located in the northwest corner of Connecticut, set high on a hill, surrounded by a golf course, and overlooked a large lake. It was breathtakingly gorgeous. It was the first year girls attended Hotchkiss and I could not believe how beautiful they were, how smart everyone was, and how good the athletics were.

For the most part my classmates were from upper middle class families (with a few global "brand names" added to the mix). To me, the remarkable thing about my classmates was how open and friendly they all were. They reminded me of the Golden Retrievers they had at home. They were always willing to approach you first and assumed, correctly, you would want to be their friend. I am not sure if this personality trait stemmed from good parenting or from never having been given a wedgie and hung from a flagpole, but I quickly decided to leave my bad attitude behind and I soon found myself with many more close friends than during my years as The New Kid.

When I would go to New York City and its suburbs on weekends to visit my friends' families, I had a slightly different feeling. I was not, as the cliché goes, standing on the outside with my nose pressed up against the glass. Instead, I was welcomed in the front door and granted every courtesy. Yet, despite my hosts' best efforts, I felt I did not really belong and intuitively understood if that was ever to change I needed to personally accomplish something. (What that might be I had no idea.)

Back at Hotchkiss, the quickest way to belong was to excel in the classroom. For the first time in my life, I was in a school environment where achievement, not goofing off, was cool. Hotchkiss was not easy for me—or for anyone. The school was consciously organized to push each student to their limit academically, athletically, and socially. Although I loved my two years at Hotchkiss, I still remember the feeling I would get in a car returning to the school after a rare weekend at home or a friend's house. I had a pit in my stomach because I knew I was going back into the belly of the beast. I would get quieter and quieter as we drove closer and closer to the school. However, once I arrived at Hotchkiss, I would hit the books hard, play my sports hard, and have a riotous good time with my new friends. In an effort for a fresh start, I decided to substitute lacrosse for baseball and, while I continued to play ice hockey, lacrosse quickly became my favorite sport. I felt good about myself and good about life…but at the end of my junior year the storm clouds returned.

After six years in Williamstown, my father was once again fired and money got real tight real fast. My parents could no longer afford for me to go to Hotchkiss and they didn't know where I would go to school because my father hadn't yet gotten another job. Since my family's first move, this was the greatest anguish I had felt in my young life. I had found a home at Hotchkiss, but I had been through this drill before and I mentally prepared myself to leave my new school when the unexpected happened. My father went to the admissions office and asked for a loan—but the school said no because they determined my family could not afford a loan. Instead, they offered me a substantial scholarship which my parents and I accepted with great relief and gratitude. A year later, with the help of the Hotchkiss lacrosse coach, I was fortunate to be admitted to Bowdoin College where I played one year of varsity hockey and four years of varsity lacrosse. (Senior year I was co-captain of the team and, fortunately for everyone, by this time I had gotten over my urge to moon people.) After a great academic, athletic and social college experience, I was (almost) ready for the big leagues.

MY PARENTS

Generations ago, my father's family had been prominent Chicago merchants who owned a large and successful business which provided supplies and equipment to commercial vessels—a ship chandlery.* However, in the early 1900s, the formerly bustling Great Lakes maritime trade began to shrink due to competition from new technology—first trains and then trucks. By the time my father came of age, the business was gone and the family money and vitality left with it. Dad was raised in an environment which was insularly focused on family and he wasn't naturally blessed with, nor given much opportunity to develop, the people skills which are so crucial in business and life.

---

*George B. Carpenter & Co.

While not particularly social, my mother's family was quite different from the Carpenters. My grandfather, Arthur VanVlissingen, was second generation Dutch. A writer by trade, he withstood the gale force headwinds of the Great Depression and provided for his family by hustling a series of jobs and by being smart, tough, and resourceful. This is also an accurate description of his eldest daughter, my mother.

Mom

As we moved from town to town, Mom assumed the job of getting her five children "launched" in the new community. Like the leader of an old-fashioned wagon train "medicine show" (selling bottles of magic elixir which in reality consisted mainly of alcohol), Mom would shamelessly oversell the abilities of her children to the teachers, coaches, or other official persons who controlled opportunities she was determined we have. While Mom often operated behind the scenes, I remember having a front row seat for one of her classic flim-flam performances.

We moved to Missouri in the spring of 1967. I was in sixth grade and in a few months the "Summer of Love" would commence with Hippies selling their beguiling magic elixir consisting of music, drugs, politics, and sexual freedom. While liking the music part, the rest of that stuff was so far over my head I barely knew it existed. Even if I had been aware of those things, I'm certain they would have been shunted aside so I could concentrate full-time worrying about the prospect of trying to make new friends in my third elementary school in two years.

My mother was also concerned about me and the impact all this moving was having on my already modest academic progress. I remember going with Mom to my new elementary school in Webster Groves for my first day. Before Mom let me out of her sight, she insisted both of us meet with the principal. We walked into a tired-looking office and introduced ourselves to a tired-looking man. Once we were all seated, the principal behind his desk and Mom and me in front, the medicine show began. Mom warmed up the audience of one by saying nice things about our new town and what *wonderful* things she had heard about the school system. Just as the principal began to relax and enjoy the pleasant company of this woman in his office, Mom got down to business.

My mother began carefully constructing a beautiful hot air balloon that represented the talents and potential of her very special sixth grade son seated next to her. This balloon floated above us and shone a soft light down like a Renaissance painting depicting the divine. While receiving no instructions, I intuitively understood my job was to remain mute lest I cause the wondrous balloon to come crashing down with an ill-timed remark. Everything appeared to be going swimmingly, until the principal opened a drawer of his desk and produced a very inconvenient sheet of paper—a transcript of grades sent to him by my school in New Hampshire.

As the principal continued to listen, I could see him looking down and struggling to square the gifted child, being so compellingly described by mother, with the decidedly mediocre record in black and white in front of him. When Mom paused for a breath, the principal attempted to gently ask about some of the glaring shortcomings on my record, but Mom was having none of that. With her eyes fixed steadily on his, she continued to extol my virtues with the unstated challenge to the principal being, *"Are you going to believe me or that piece of paper?"* Finally, with a heavy sigh, I saw the principal give up trying to reconcile the irreconcilable. After a few more minutes, and a few more sighs, the principal decided discretion was the better part of valor and I was granted fast track status for all classes.

This was quintessential Mom—flattering, arguing, cajoling, and insisting the powers that be, with authority over her children, work with her to achieve the Carpenter family's hopes and dreams. There were many times the Carpenter children, and occasionally the powers that be, fell down on the job. These instances were much to my mother's chagrin, however, on this issue Mom was an unstoppable force; never meeting an obstacle she felt she couldn't overcome—with her children firmly in tow.

Unfortunately, there was one thing my mother's determination could not make right. When I was a freshman in college, my parents got divorced. Dad never shared his feelings with me about this event, but Mom did. With great sorrow in her voice she said, "*I love your father, but I just can't stay married to someone who doesn't have the capacity to reciprocate emotionally.*" There was no good guy or bad guy in this tragedy—just two people who always loved their family, still loved each other, but who after a certain period of time could no longer live together.

Early on, my hope was that divorce would be the right answer for the two people I loved most. If it could bring my parents even a modicum of relief and happiness I was all for it. However, looking back, it seems when Mom and Dad were together life was a struggle, and whey they divorced life was still a struggle. After 30 years of marriage, I don't think there was a right answer.

Dad

During the writing of this book my father died. As far as I know, during his entire life, Dad never had one single friend. He had family, co-workers and acquaintances, but no friends. However, I don't think he felt that as a loss. Friendship simply wasn't something his constitution needed or even could accommodate. Despite being solitary, my father was a wonderful man and father. The one group of people who could break through and find a light and playful side of Dad were young children—especially his own. When the five of us were little, Dad gave us all pet names. My older sister, Lindsey, was "Linny Bell Brown"; I was "B. Benderman Bug"; Arthur was "Arturo Good Boy Duck Quack Quack"; and the twins, Helen and Frances, were "Helka-Pie" and "Fadal." While Dad always loved us, it seemed as we got older, we (along with everyone else) became the kind of complicated equations he had little ability to understand and even less to solve. It's both pleasurable and painful remembering back to those days when Dad found happiness being with his young family, all the while knowing of the struggles in front of him—and now he is gone.

In addition to his other positive traits, Dad was *always* a gentleman (in every sense of the word) and his integrity was as much a part of him as any vital organ. A striking example of Dad's character was a story concerning my older sister, Lindsey. We were living in Williamstown and Lindsey was a sophomore in college and home for Christmas vacation. It was mid-morning, December 26, and Lindsey was the passenger in her high school girlfriend's VW Bug. Lindsey and her friend, Jamie Haig, were using the excuse of exchanging Christmas presents in town as a reason to get together and catch up. The day was sunny and the pavement was dry.

As the road followed a beautiful winding stream, Jaime and Lindsey rounded a bend and saw another VW Bug approaching from the opposite direction. Just as the two Bugs were about to pass, a large black dog ran out in front of the other Bug and the driver swerved head-on into Jamie and Lindsey. The collision of the Bugs was absolute. Both were traveling 55 mph and, because there was no time to break, the vehicles absorbed 100 percent of the impact. It was as if each car drove into a wall of steel at 110 mph.

Miraculously, Lindsey was okay. She had her seat belt and shoulder harness on and, although knocked unconscious, her only other serious injury was a broken collar bone from the shoulder harness that undoubtedly saved her life. Jamie didn't have her seat belt on and sustained multiple life-threatening injuries, but after six months in the hospital and losing four inches off her shattered left leg, she did ultimately recover. The driver of the other Bug, a young woman also in her early 20s who was on her way to work at a nursing home, died immediately. To complete the tragedy, the Labrador Retriever, which the other driver swerved to avoid, was obliterated between the front ends of the two Bugs.

A few days after Lindsey's accident, I was still on Christmas break from Hotchkiss and returned home late one afternoon to find Mom and Dad in the living room, talking to a strange man. This was an unusual sight because my parents rarely entertained. I was introduced to the man, but it was clear I was not being invited to join the conversation. I shook his hand and walked into the kitchen, but instead of embarking on my daily, futile, search for a snack, I hung around the door to the living room watching and listening. I quickly realized this man was an "ambulance chaser"—a lawyer looking to drum up personal injury business. The lawyer began to explain, since the accident was the fault of the other driver, our family could sue the driver's family *"for large monetary pain and suffering damages."* He further explained that while the girl and her parents had few assets, there were grandparents who did have means and he believed he could somehow get them to pay.

Once my father heard enough to understand the lawyer's plan, he stood up and said softly, but with clear hard emotion, *"That girl is dead and we are not going to be suing anyone. It was an accident and now it is time for you to leave."* Not waiting for the lawyer to respond, Dad walked to the front door, opened it, and ushered him out. The last words I heard the lawyer say as the front door closed were, *"If you change your mind, call me…"*

A few short months later was when Dad lost his job and I thought I was going to have to leave Hotchkiss. At that time our family's financial situation was getting desperate. However, my father's integrity was such he would have chosen to be penniless rather than solve his financial problems by doing something he believed to be unethical—like suing that girl's family.

The final five years of Dad's life were an inexorable slide into the clutches of dementia. When he died, it was a blessing. It seems a cruel symmetry that my father, whose personality isolated him from others, was afflicted with a disease which, before it kills, isolates its victims from themselves by destroying their memories.

Dad's notable talents and shortcomings created a unique combination of challenges for him. I am proud and eternally grateful to my father that every time he was knocked down he got back up and kept fighting for us. In addition to my father, Leigh's father died recently. My mother is doing well and still going strong, but Leigh's mother recently suffered a stroke and has moved in with us. I realize, as Avery is going through her passage into the real world, Leigh and I are going through our own passage—separating from our parents for the last time.

BENJER

Benjer was my name growing up. When we first moved from Illinois, that name ceased being used outside our family and, gradually, it died out there as well. However, I still like to think of myself as a Benjer because it reminds me of the fun childhood my parents worked so hard to provide. Over the past few years, Benjer made a brief comeback as my father's dementia robbed him of all except his early memories. Each time my father called me Benjer, it first made me smile and then want to cry.

As the parents of my generation leave us, and that firewall to our mortality is gone, it is a natural time to take stock of one's life. I know my integrity is not as pure as my father's and my determination is not as strong as my mother's. However, I appreciate how fortunate

I was to have both my parents as role models. I was also fortunate for the ways my childhood experiences prepared me for the real world. Not because of any master plan (of mine or anyone else's), I was often forced to sell myself to new people in new situations and it gave me the sensibilities of an outsider. Finally, the fear of financial ruin haunted my family like a boogeyman who would regularly appear, then recede, only to reappear. A deep-seated fear of the boogeyman, and a desperate desire to find a stable place in the world, have been the two sharp spurs which have driven me forward.

Part One
How to Survive, Thrive, and Have
Fun in the Big Leagues

Chapter 1

Managing a Corporate Career

My career was not a straight line up. I experienced a significant number of setbacks and detours along the way. While you can learn some lessons from my successes, you can learn even more from my mistakes and failures. Let's start at the beginning.

FIRST AT BAT

I remember my first "Welcome to the big leagues" moment vividly. When my senior year of college came around, I didn't know what I wanted to do. Being a government major, I thought someday I might go to law school. At that moment, however, I just wanted to get a job where I could learn something about business, make some money, and hopefully keep having fun. During the winter term, I went to the Bowdoin College Career Services Office and introduced myself to the office head who was an old school New England gentleman.

The Head and I hit it off immediately and, after a few meetings, I could tell he was in my corner. The Head told me he thought I would do great in banking, and he said I was in luck because J.P. Morgan was coming to do on-campus interviews. Though all the interview spots were taken, The Head told me he was going to squeeze me in. He further explained J.P. Morgan came to Bowdoin every year to recruit and he knew the Morgan Guys very well. Back in the early 80s, J.P. Morgan was considered to be the gold standard of commercial banks. While not explaining much to me, The Head did communicate the high regard he had for this company.

As luck would have it, J.P. Morgan was the first bank to interview on campus and, less than a week after my talk with The Head, I found myself putting on my Sunday best (from my days of living at home and being forced to go to church with my mother). By this time, my Sunday best was at least six years old and consisted of a pair of gray flannel pants, a full three inches too short, and a tweed jacket easily two sizes too small. While more than a little physically uncomfortable due to my ill-fitting clothes, I walked across campus to Career Services with a spring in my step and brimming with confidence borne of ignorance.

When it was my turn, I walked into the conference room and gave a firm handshake to my interviewer, a Morgan Guy, who graduated from Bowdoin a few years earlier. After a few quick pleasantries he got down to business:

Morgan Guy: *So, why are you interested in banking?*

Me (being ridiculously honest): *Actually, I hadn't thought much about it, but The Head said he thought I would be good at it.*

Morgan Guy (probably feeling stunned by my honesty and naiveté, but willing to give me another chance): *Okay…what do you think might be appealing to you about banking?*

Me (if nothing else showing consistency): *I'm really not sure; I was hoping you could tell me about the business.*

I had just given the Morgan Guy irrefutable confirmation I was every bit as stupid as I looked, and I am sure he was distressed to realize he had no choice but to waste 20 minutes of his life humoring me. On the other side of the table, I was convinced I was handling my first interview like a seasoned pro. At the end, we stood up and I gave the Morgan Guy another vigorous handshake. I left feeling pretty darn good, mentally high-fiving myself and thinking, "*I nailed it!*"

The next day I went to see The Head in his office to hear the good news. But when I walked in he looked like his dog had just died. He told me he was very sorry but J.P. Morgan didn't think I was ready to be a banker. He looked so sad I felt bad for *him*! I told The Head it wasn't his fault and I would try to get myself ready—whatever that meant.

Like having a 90 mph fastball thrown at me, my experience with the Morgan Guy was a major wake-up call. In retrospect, it was the best thing that could have happened and it was the beginning of what has been a 33-year journey to discover what works, and what doesn't work, in the big leagues.

FIRST JOB SEARCH

Despite my failure to generate any interest from the Morgan Guy, I did learn a great deal from that experience. While there are some new technologies that can be helpful in your job search, the most important dynamic—effective personal networking—hasn't changed much since the dawn of capitalism. What has changed is the quality of the competition. You need to be much better prepared and conduct a much more thorough and professional search than I did 30 years ago. Just like professional sports, the quality of the competition keeps getting better.

While I give The Head low marks for preparing me for my interviews, I give him high marks for suggesting I look into banking. I quickly realized banking would give me exposure to many companies and how they operate. This appealed to me, so I devised my own plan for getting a job. First, I got a list of recent Bowdoin graduates from Career Services who were working in banking in New York, and I went to visit them in the big city. I had a dozen informational interviews with these junior bankers and began to get pretty excited. All these Bowdoin grads appeared to be "locked and loaded." They loved living in New York and seemed excited about their jobs. They had left behind the laid-back college environment and there was a crispness and confidence to the way they looked, talked, and walked. I wanted to be one of them.

Superman

After being out of the job market for 12 years while raising her five children, my mother, using her Wellesley degree and well-practiced sales skills, landed a job as the Director of Development at Montclair Kimberly Academy (an independent day school in New Jersey). In this role she had a good deal of interaction with the MKA Board of Trustees. One of them, whom I will call Superman, was a senior banker at Bankers Trust Company in Manhattan. One Friday, with my job search in full swing, Mom ran into Superman and asked if he would be willing to talk to me about banking. Superman said, "*Sure, have your son in my office with a suit on Monday morning.*" Mom was excited but concerned because she knew I was preparing for exams, and she said something about me maybe not being able to get from Maine to New York on such short notice. Superman, clearly feeling great sympathy for my situation, growled "*You didn't hear me Carol…tell him to get to my office Monday morning.*"

On Monday morning, Superman's assistant greeted me and I took a seat outside his office. I didn't know what to expect. At this point I had only spoken to junior bankers, either in New York or at Bowdoin, so I had no idea what a "real" banker looked like. Finally,

Superman's office door opened and three young bankers hurled themselves out the door almost at a dead run. I soon found out why.

As I entered his office, my impression of Superman was that he was younger than I imagined, around 40 years old. Physically, he shared little in common with his namesake. He was about 5′8″, balding, and it did not appear a spandex costume would look flattering on him. Nevertheless, his energy level and confidence were off the charts and, in my wide-eyed state, he seemed as if he just might be *able to leap tall buildings in a single bound*. Also startling was Superman's spacious office which looked like an ambitious architect's small-scale model of a futuristic Metropolis. Every flat surface was covered with clear Lucite tombstones, 6 to 18 inches tall, memorializing the financial deals Superman used his powers to transact.

Superman started our meeting by slapping me on the back as if I had something caught in my throat he was trying to dislodge. Then, as we were shaking hands, he basically threw me into a chair before I could recover from his version of the Heimlich maneuver. He peppered me with questions, kept interrupting me halfway through my answers, and after 15 minutes he jumped up, said "*Let's go*," and marched out of his office at only a slightly slower pace than the three junior bankers a few minutes earlier.

As I trailed behind, Superman passed by the elevators to the emergency stairwell, jogged briskly down three flights of stairs, before coming out to an area with a sign that said, "Human Resources." Superman grabbed the first person he saw in HR, pointed at me and commanded, "*This kid seems ok, I want you to talk to him.*" After giving me one more super slap on the back, he headed out the door of HR at the walking equivalent of flying.

After that superhero experience, my interview with the HR staffer was unremarkable. I soon found myself back on Park Avenue, with cars and people whizzing around me, not really understanding

what just happened. Two weeks later I received a thin envelope
from Bankers Trust which explained everything I needed to know:
I was offered a job in their commercial lending training program!
In retrospect, what happened was I had the right contact (my
mother), with the right guy (Superman), at the right time (I had
failed enough, and learned enough, in my job search to be ready to
effectively sell myself in a professional context). The result was I got a
great job.

I know I was lucky to get good career advice from The Head and
an interview arranged by my mother. On the other hand, I received
no advice on how to go about my job search or how to prepare for an
interview. All in all, I was fortunate to receive the help I got and you
may not be as fortunate. Regardless, maybe for the first time in your
life, *you are in charge and it is up to you to do whatever it takes to get a
great job.* While you can hope for the best (getting a great job reasonably quickly), you should prepare for the worst—a drawn-out
campaign with much hand-to-hand combat, before you finally get
a great job. You need a battle plan, and the good news is you're holding it in your hands. Chapter 7 of *The Bigs* is everything you need to
know and—if executed with intelligence and energy—you *will* win
the war and get a great job.

FIRST JOB

Before I could become a junior banker, I needed to pass Bankers
Trust's commercial lending training program. The best part of
the program was getting to know my 20 trainee classmates. The
worst part of the program, for me, was the intensive crash course
in accounting. I didn't dislike accounting, but as a government
major, I just didn't get the hang of it very quickly. It soon felt like
this crash course would crash my career before I even got started.
I felt an enormous amount of pressure because I realized if I failed

accounting, I would wash out of the program and be forced to move to New Jersey and live with my mother and my younger twin sisters. Having witnessed the pain my father endured from his professional failures, I was terrified to feel history beginning to repeat itself.

I vividly remember the days leading up to our final accounting exam. After classes, I stayed alone at the training center studying late into the night. The training center was located high up in Bankers Trust's downtown office tower, which was next to the World Trade Centers and near Wall Street. Occasionally, I would look out the window at the masses of people, who looked like ants, swarming around the subway entrance on their way home. I remember asking myself, "*Am I really dumber than all those tiny people down there who are gainfully employed?*" Fortunately, and narrowly, the answer turned out to be "*no*" and I somehow passed the test which allowed me to graduate from the training program. I was assigned to Bankers Trust's Empire State Building branch.

The Professor and Me

The Professor was my first real boss and he was a good one. He looked like the Professor on *Gilligan's Island* (but always in a perfectly tailored suit) and was just as intelligent (though in entirely different ways). While the Professor on TV was a mechanical genius who could make a radio out of coconuts, my boss was the most erudite and cultured man I ever met. He was deeply involved with the New York City arts world and had only a modest interest in banking. The Professor, however, was so intelligent that with only 25 percent of his attention he still knew more about banking than anyone else in the office. The task of our Empire State Building branch was to lend money to the "rag trade" (the clothing and fashion industry) which was located in that area of Manhattan.

The Professor and I got along great, and I loved going along on sales calls and watching him charm clients with his wit, knowledge,

and winning personality. I think The Professor understood how
much I respected his talents and enjoyed learning from him.
(By the way, that is *always* a solid foundation on which to build a
positive relationship with your boss!) The problem was, the more
comfortable I became *in* my job as a banker the less comfortable
I became *with* my job as a banker. Although I learned a great deal
about the business, I came to view my branch as a backwater. The
brightest guy in the office, The Professor, was not fully engaged and
the less bright guys were just that. Nobody seemed very "amped up"
about the whole enterprise.

After I had been at the office 18 months, The Professor, for
the first time, found fault with my performance when he came
down hard on me about entertainment expenses. It seems I was
undermining the entire Bankers Trust operation at the Empire
State Building branch because I was not spending *enough* money on
entertainment and if I didn't *shape up quickly*, we ran the risk of having our entertainment budget cut. The Professor's admonishment
to spend more money entertaining was not in order to generate
more business; he was worried that our entertainment budget might
get cut. This pushed me over the edge and I realized that I needed
to go out and find a job where the best and the brightest were fully
engaged in trying to maximize, not milk, their career opportunities.

I enjoyed the commercial lending business, but perhaps most
importantly, realized being a corporate lawyer was not for me. I liked
meeting with clients, learning about their businesses, and structur-
ing loans which would satisfy their needs in ways that would give
Bankers Trust a high likelihood of being repaid with interest. At that
point, the lawyers were brought in to "paper" the deal (i.e., write the
loan documents) and I knew I didn't want to spend my career handling the paperwork for someone else's deal.

Although I decided to leave commercial lending, I didn't
know what I wanted to do. I thought my banking client contacts

might lead me to a small firm with potential to grow, but no such opportunity presented itself. What did present itself was a raucous party on Wall Street that was just getting cranked up.

A historic 30-year bull market in stocks and bonds, which began almost exactly when I graduated from college two years earlier, was starting to roar. However, from my low perch at the bottom of the Empire State Building, I could barely hear the noise. While I knew virtually nothing about Wall Street, from snippets of conversations I heard when out and about socially, I came to understand the people involved in sales and trading worked together in large rooms, traded stocks and bonds by yelling at each other, and made lots of money. That was good enough for me. I wanted in on the party and I asked The Professor if he would support my efforts to transfer to the sales and trading department of Bankers Trust.

From the first day I showed up at the Empire State Building, The Professor had been nothing but a terrific boss. He patiently taught me everything he knew about banking and made it fun to learn. The Professor invested a great deal of time and effort in me, and I knew he would be disappointed I wanted to leave. However, consistent with being a terrific boss, when I told him my plan he immediately said it sounded like a *great idea* and I had his *full support*. The only problem was getting transferred to the sales and trading department downtown was not under his control. I needed to get the blessing of HR and then interview for a job.

A few days later, I made my way uptown to headquarters. The woman in HR listened to my plan and then said, "*Your boss has given you a great recommendation and I will do everything I can to help you get a job downtown in sales and trading.*" Before I could break out the party hats and confetti, she said in the next breath, "*All you have to do is stay working at the Empire State Building for three more years.*" This caught me off guard, but I quickly gathered myself and responded,

*"I will give you two months to help me get transferred, and then I am
going to start interviewing at other banks."* A few weeks later, I was
taking the subway downtown every morning to my new job on the
trading floor of Bankers Trust.

SOMETHING BETTER OUT THERE

Working as a U.S. Treasury bond salesman at Bankers Trust was
more fun than I had even imagined. While I knew little about what I
was getting into, I was correct everyone was in a large room shouting
at each other. I was also correct a job like that would be perfect for
me. As with many businesses, when I first arrived on the trading
floor, it seemed everyone was speaking a foreign language. However,
everything was held together by the logic of making money and
I soon got into the swing of things.

In some ways, I may have felt too comfortable on the Bankers
Trust trading floor. After three years, I started to feel as I had with
commercial lending: There was something bigger and better out
there for me. Specifically, I thought a few of the larger trading firms
might offer more opportunity for career advancement and higher
compensation.

I focused on two firms, First Boston (now Credit Suisse) and
Morgan Stanley, because most people at Bankers Trust seemed to
regard them as the best in the business. My idea was to join one of
these firms as a Treasury bond salesman and then move into selling
corporate bonds (which, at that time, was a business Bankers Trust
didn't do). Both firms offered me jobs, but Morgan Stanley had
better accounts for me to cover.

Just before my final decision, I got an unexpected call from a former Bankers Trust colleague. My friend had recently joined a small
firm: Greenwich Capital. What he told me was music to my ears; his
new firm was kicking ass, taking names, and laughing all the way to

the bank. After a single interview at Greenwich Capital, I was sold. I was about to accept a job offer when things changed dramatically.

Greenwich Capital got caught on the wrong side of what was to become one of the most infamous trades in the history of the U.S. Treasury bond market—forever known as "9 $1/4$, 9 $7/8$"—after the coupons of the two affected bonds. The details of the trade are not important, but the result was Greenwich Capital lost a very significant amount of money and the joke around Wall Street was the firm was going to have to change its name to "*Greenwich No Capital.*"

Not surprisingly, I decided Morgan Stanley would be a more stable place to work and I accepted that job. There were no hard feelings at Greenwich Capital over my decision because they had gone into survival mode—which didn't include hiring a mid-level salesman. In business, however, things can change quickly and Greenwich Capital soon regained its footing and went back to its winning ways. I, on the other hand, quickly began to regret my decision to join Morgan Stanley.

Entrepreneurial opportunities and environments have always appealed to me. Morgan Stanley was then, and is now, an outstanding firm. However, as with most large and successful companies, there also comes a certain amount of corporate formality which was not a perfect fit for me. So, after less than a year at Morgan Stanley, I knew I wanted to move again—but where and doing what? My entrepreneurial itch led me to make a dramatic decision. I was going to leave my Wall Street career behind and become a full-time nightclub owner. While this certainly was a radical decision, it wasn't quite as "out of left field" as it sounds.

Through an unusual set of circumstances (which I will explain in the next chapter), when I first moved to Manhattan six years earlier, I became involved as an owner of a bar (this was a side interest to my day job at Bankers Trust). This experience focused my attention on the commercial opportunities in the nightlife entertainment business, and I felt I had a "can't miss" idea. It was clear to me most big nightclubs were not particularly welcoming to young professionals. The image and clientele the nightclubs embraced was more hip and edgy. My idea was to create a nightclub where young professionals would feel at home, know they would run into friends, and be able to talk since the music wouldn't be played at ear-splitting decibels. At that time, the greatest concentration of young professionals lived on the Upper East Side, but I couldn't find the kind of space I was looking for there. I decided to go to the other stomping ground of these young professionals—Wall Street.

When I moved from Bankers Trust to Morgan Stanley, I left downtown for midtown. However, I spent three years working downtown and I understood the Wall Street after-work scene. My plan was to capture the young professionals when they left work between 5 p.m. (for sales and trading) and 10 p.m. (for investment banking). I would get the party rolling early and the after-work crowd would tag team with the late crowd (which would consist of other young professionals looking for a night on the town). Since my crowd would start arriving early, this would avoid an enormously expensive chicken-and-egg problem all nightclubs are afflicted with—no one wants to go, or be, somewhere that's empty. The result is nightclub crowds arrive ridiculously late and these lost hours can never be recouped. With this business plan, I felt confident that I could more than double the revenue of a typical nightclub.

I focused my efforts to find space near the South Street Seaport because what little bar scene the Wall Street area had was concentrated there. Happily, there was a decent supply of available real estate in the area and it didn't take long to find a spot I loved. It was an ancient warehouse, steps away from the East River, on a cobblestone street, in the shadows of the Brooklyn Bridge. The minute I entered this picturesque yet rugged space, I could picture it as my bar/nightclub/restaurant. The area was known as Peck

Slip, which provided the name of my new establishment: The Slip. I negotiated an option on the lease, lined up the $1 million needed to renovate the warehouse (from two real estate investors I had been introduced to through friends), and was about to resign from Morgan Stanley when my wife, Leigh, inserted herself into this decision in a major way.

I had met Leigh Worcester 10 years earlier when she was a freshman and I was a sophomore at Bowdoin. It was a classic case of love (or at least lust) at first sight. Of course, I'm describing my reaction when I saw her at a party—I'm pretty certain that first innocent meeting meant a whole lot less to Leigh at the time. After college, Leigh had gotten a master's degree from Columbia's School of Journalism, was working in public relations in New York, and we had been married two years. By now, Leigh was used to my crazy entrepreneurial ideas. However, having me involved in owning a bar as a secondary business to my primary Wall Street career was one thing; being married to a full-time nightclub owner was something else entirely. Leigh argued that I liked the business of sales and trading; I just didn't enjoy working at Morgan Stanley. So why not move to a different firm rather than make a truly radical career move? Also, while our marriage was terrific, Leigh did mention she wasn't too keen about me being out every night until 4:00 a.m.

I was taken aback by how negatively Leigh felt about my new career plans and I started to reconsider. I tried to sell my investors that I could help run The Slip on the side while continuing my Wall Street career. However, they didn't buy that pitch. The investors had committed to The Slip because they believed in my vision and my full-time commitment to work to realize that vision. I had to choose between my wife's wishes and the nightclub. After a few days of soul-searching, I called my friend at Greenwich Capital and, after just one more interview, I agreed to join the young upstart firm.

ONLY YOU CAN LOOK OUT FOR YOURSELF

Before I could start at Greenwich Capital, I needed to resign from Morgan Stanley, which I assumed would not be too difficult since I had been there only 10 months. I was wrong. My sales manager reacted to my resignation with anger and seemed to view it as a personal affront. He sent me straight away to see John Mack. Mack was the Head of Fixed Income and eight years later would become the CEO of Morgan Stanley.

Mack Attack

I was ushered into Mack's office and he was right out of central casting—a big man in a big office. During the brief opening round of pleasantries, I could feel Mack sizing me up like a professional prizefighter against a lesser opponent. Being a pro, however, Mack took nothing for granted. After gliding confidently around the ring a few times, he settled on a plan of attack and started swinging—not wildly—but with deliberate and measured blows. A right jab, *"you're making a huge mistake"*…a left jab, *"that firm is too small"*…setting me up for a right uppercut, *"you will regret this."*

For 10 minutes, Mack worked me over the best he could. However, by that time I was six years into my career, had already changed jobs twice, and Mack's punches didn't faze me. When he paused to catch his breath, I calmly explained my mind was made up. Mack didn't like the fact I had effectively taken charge of the fight and sent him back to his corner. When I left Mack's office a few moments later, he was in a decidedly less good mood than when I entered.

While it would be a stretch to say I won anything that day, what is true is that I went a few rounds with a veteran Wall Street brawler and left the ring unbloodied and unbowed, with my head held high, and an even greater conviction I could succeed in this game. With hindsight and without a doubt, the career advice John Mack gave me that day was spectacularly bad and thank goodness I ignored it. Over the next 20 years that "*too small*" firm, Greenwich Capital, became one of the most highly regarded and profitable firms on Wall Street. Also, everything about the structure and culture of that small firm fit me perfectly.

I don't believe for a second John Mack cared about what was best for me. He only cared about what was best for Morgan Stanley. I didn't then, and I don't now, hold that against him. It is, however, a perfect example of how you need to look after your own career interests because no one else is going to do it for you.

WHAT I DID RIGHT—WHAT I DID WRONG

The early part of my career highlights two important lessons about what I did right and what I did wrong in managing my career. My move from commercial lending to sales and trading was a great example of a positive lesson: *Don't be patient*. While it may make sense for you to stay in your first job a little longer than you want in order to build your resume, do not get stuck in a job that won't allow you to achieve your professional and personal goals. There are plenty of companies and jobs out there; go find one that is a great fit for you.

My move from Bankers Trust sales and trading to Morgan Stanley was an equally great example of a negative lesson: *Don't leap before looking*. I had been at Bankers Trust for six years, had gone through Bankers Trust's two primary training programs (commercial lending and sales and trading), and I had a strong network of friends throughout the bank. I also knew that senior people on the Bankers Trust trading floor liked me. So why leave?

I thought becoming a corporate bond salesman at Morgan Stanley (which back then was one of the most glamorous sales jobs in the business) would be a good career move, but I did no research to confirm that. My plan was to get a job at Morgan Stanley as a Treasury bond salesman and then transfer into the corporate bond sales department. Unfortunately, there were two major flaws in my plan.

- First, after I had been at Morgan Stanley for a few months, I realized I had little interest in selling corporate bonds! Because of their relative illiquidity, a corporate salesman often has to sell the inventory his traders already own. For Treasury bonds, because of their high liquidity, virtually any trade can be executed because the bonds are always available. The freedom to sell whatever ideas and bonds I liked was the primary reason I enjoyed selling Treasuries.

- Second, my direct boss at Morgan Stanley didn't seem to care about me or about anyone else in the department. If I had wanted to stay at Morgan Stanley and move from selling Treasuries to selling corporates, I doubt I could have gotten his support. All he seemed to care about was for the U.S. Treasury department to perform well so he could move on to his next big job at Morgan Stanley.

Leigh has always said one of my greatest weaknesses is being too impetuous—and she's right. Since I was going to Morgan Stanley with a plan to become a corporate bond salesman, I should have talked to professionals (both inside and outside Morgan Stanley) who were doing that job to see if I actually would like it. Also, I could easily have done some networking and asked people at Morgan Stanley about my new boss. I now understand how fortunate I was in my career to bounce around and end up at Greenwich Capital. You cannot count on being so lucky. Always be impatient and willing to jump into new opportunities, but always research these new opportunities thoroughly *before* your feet leave the ground.

TED

Despite its modest size, my new firm was well-known on the Bankers Trust and Morgan Stanley trading floors. As one of the co-founders of Greenwich Capital, Ted Knetzger was already a "name" on Wall Street. Ted graduated from the University of Virginia where he played soccer and headed to Wall Street to find his fame and fortune. After an unremarkable eight years at Kidder Peabody, Ted, at age 30, had the temerity to decide he wanted to start his own firm. My favorite story Ted tells of the early days is when he and the other founding partner of Greenwich Capital, Bill Rainer, would race to be first to arrive at their one-room office because the only furniture they had were two folding lawn chairs and one had a nasty habit of periodically collapsing without warning!

Like any world-class salesman, Ted had an abundance of charisma and determination. Every great salesman, however, also needs a great product to sell—and that product was Ted's vision for Greenwich Capital. Ted's vision was that, unlike the rest of Wall Street, *his* firm's #1 priority would be to help employees realize their hopes and dreams—which hopefully would result in a handsome return for the firm's owners. It was a unique and ambitious plan, but over the next 28 years Greenwich Capital accomplished just that for thousands of employees and the firm's owners.

When I first met Ted in 1987, he was in his mid-30s. Even then his good looks could be fairly described as distinguished. The best comparison, in today's terms, is he looked like a younger version of the Dos Equis "Most Interesting Man in the World." My favorite thing about Ted was his laugh. When Ted found something amusing (which was often), his laugh would start somewhere deep inside and quickly burst to the surface as if it had been starved for oxygen. Ted's laugh was so spontaneous, so loud, and so natural, he often made a large room full of people smile even if only a few heard the joke or story.

While Ted was highly intelligent, he never seemed to care if people recognized it. All Ted seemed to care about was making sure *you* knew he thought *you* were intelligent. If you want someone to like you, this is a great way to start.

As a salesman, Ted was without peer. Every salesman knew if he could get Ted out on the golf course with a client that client would become a fan of Greenwich Capital for life. Clients loved Ted because he loved them. The truth is Ted loved everyone. As a testament to how fascinated everyone at Greenwich Capital was with Ted, if you ever wanted to get someone's attention all you needed to say was, "*I was with Ted yesterday and we…*" With that preamble, you not only would get one person's attention, but everyone within earshot would edge closer to hear the story.

Over the years, I have heard people describe Ted as "fun," "interesting," "thoughtful," "gregarious," "humble," "honest," "charming," "gentle," "instinctive," and "warm." While I agree with all of those, for me, the word that best describes Ted's most outstanding character trait is "generous." Ted was as happy to be with senior employees (his old friends) as with junior employees who had joined the company that week. If you worked at Greenwich Capital you were Ted's friend, and he genuinely wanted to get to know you and have some fun together.

Professionally, Ted was equally generous. I experienced his enormous generosity for the first time in 1988 after I had been at Greenwich Capital less than a year. Ted announced the company was being bought by Long Term Credit Bank (LTCB), a large Japanese bank. In these types of transactions key employees are typically given contracts to retain their services and as recognition of their help in building the company. Since I was a new mid-level employee, I expected nothing. However, days after the transaction was announced, Ted asked me to come by his office. When I did he told me what a "*great job*" I had been doing (believe me, I just got there, it couldn't have been all that great) and he had "*put me down*" for a contract which would pay me additional compensation equal to three times what I was going to make that year. In essence, I was being paid for three years of work I didn't do! As if that wasn't enough, after the LTCB transaction was completed, I, and others, received a handwritten note from Ted, encased in Lucite, mentioning what he saw as our individual contributions to the firm.

I remember, years later, discussing the LTCB transaction with a senior trader at the company who was involved with the deal. He said Ted could have kept the lion's share of the LTCB retention money for himself, but instead he insisted it get spread out to his employees. While the trader related this story, he kept shaking his head in a way that described, better than words, his amazement at Ted's enormous generosity.

Despite all his accomplishments and sophistication, Ted's lightness of spirit seemed to create a halo of innocence around him which drew people to him. During my time at Greenwich Capital, Ted got separated and then divorced. This appeared to make his friends even more protective of Ted—as if we would all lose something precious and irreplaceable if Ted ever stopped being Ted. In my life, I have never seen so many people root so hard for someone so successful.

Ted's Company

When I joined Greenwich Capital it was a small, 70 employee, institutional broker-dealer.* Despite its size, Greenwich Capital's business model brought the firm into direct competition with the largest Wall Street firms. Started by Ted and Bill in 1981, with $10 mm of private capital, the firm was sold to LTCB in 1988. In 1996, the firm was sold again, this time to National Westminster

---

*A broker-dealer is a firm whose business is to buy or sell securities (which primarily consist of stocks and bonds) with clients.

Bank (NatWest). Finally, in 2000, NatWest was taken over by the Royal Bank of Scotland (RBS). Due to Greenwich Capital's strong financial performance, each new parent company allowed our firm to operate with great autonomy because no one wanted to kill the goose that was laying the golden eggs! All great organizations need a set of guiding principles that form a solid foundation to build on. While Ted never wrote an official Magna Carta laying out the principles underpinning Greenwich Capital, everyone at the firm understood what his company stood for:

- *Employees always come first*: Without great employees you can't have a great company. You attract the best people by doing everything in your power to make your company a place where employees' dreams can come true.

- *Execution over strategy*: It matters less what you do than that you do it with conviction, energy, and enthusiasm. Of course you want to make good strategic decisions and focus your efforts on the most promising initiatives. However, Ted was crystal clear that he would rather have outstanding execution of a mediocre plan than mediocre execution of an outstanding plan. Greenwich Capital was very much in a "people business" and Ted believed if he had talented employees, striving to perform as all-stars, his firm would survive and thrive.

- *Compete hard at the highest level*: As an institutional broker-dealer, Greenwich Capital dealt only with professional money managers, hedge funds, insurance companies, banks, central banks, and the like—no individuals. In most cases, our clients were many times larger than our firm. Also, these clients were the most experienced, had access to the most information, and on a daily basis transacted with many of our Wall Street competitors. Dealing only with this elite universe of the most sophisticated clients was very challenging, but if you did a great job for them they also traded the most bonds.

- *Personal accountability*: When possible, tie employee compensation to individual performance. Virtually all Greenwich Capital's competitors (the major Wall Street banks and investment banks) paid subjectively. In practice, this meant our competitors paid their employees the minimum they could and still retain their services. Ted believed his performance-based pay system incentivized salespeople and traders to perform their best, reduced the politicking around compensation that was rampant on Wall Street, attracted the best and the brightest, was the fairest way to decide who got how much, and meant that a salesman or trader's compensation was limited only by the size of their contribution to the firm. Ted's compensation system was not only a throwback to the old days of Wall Street, like most good ideas, it was strikingly simple.

- *Celebrate all employee contributions*: Not everyone can be a star, either because they don't have the ability or, more likely, because their current job doesn't allow them to have a major impact on the firm's performance. Nevertheless, the value and the performance of the company is the sum of its parts. Everyone needs to do his job to the best of his abilities and be celebrated and thanked for his efforts.

- *Have fun*: Everyone spends too much time at work to not have fun. Work is serious business, but that doesn't mean you can't have a very good time doing it. You can and you should. Not surprisingly, people loved to work for Ted and they loved to work at his company.

An example of Ted's focus on personal accountability occurred early in my career at Greenwich Capital. Some developments in the U.S. Treasury bond market, and on our trading desk, raised the question of whether the sales force should continue to be paid on commission from their sales—or be paid a percentage of the money the traders generated. A meeting was held and valid arguments on both sides were presented. Halfway through, Ted walked in and sat down. He listened for two or three minutes and then, addressing the salespeople in the room, asked: "*Do you guys want to be warriors or do you just want to carry the spears?*"

Ted's analogy wasn't perfect and I *know* he didn't understand the subtleties of the issues being discussed. However, once Ted made his position clear, there was nothing left to say. The meeting adjourned and we all, quite happily, returned to our desks—still on commission and now proud to be "Ted's Warriors!"

My former sales partner at Greenwich Capital, Doug Marzonie, told a similar Ted story. Doug was an outstanding college athlete and the definition of a hyper-competitive guy. He joined Greenwich just a few months after I did. While Doug was being recruited by Ted, he asked if he could get a "*guarantee*" for the next year. (A guarantee is common on Wall Street—it means you are guaranteed to make a certain amount of money for the first year or two when you join a firm. A guarantee is offered to top talent to encourage them to take the risk of switching firms.) Ted's response, alluding to his performance-driven commission system, played to Doug's competitive ego and was pure genius: "*Sure Marz, I'll give you a guarantee… I guarantee that you will make a shitload of money if you're half as good as you think you are.*" Marz was and he did.

In a people business, recruiting is like fishing; every firm is constantly trolling for the big catch. At Greenwich Capital, with Ted's principles firmly in place and some success under our belts, fishing for all-star talent became ridiculously easy. The trophy fish, the star producers all Wall Street firms want to hire, would swarm around our boat hoping to be allowed to jump in!

There are many lessons to be learned from Ted and it is difficult to know where to start and where to stop. So, I will simply say, if you conduct yourself with a fraction of the grace, poise, honesty, intelligence, and generosity of Ted you will greatly increase your chances of accomplishing your goals—which should include having a great deal of fun!

MORE CURVEBALLS

When I joined Greenwich Capital, I was 30 years old, married for two years, and planning to start a family. My seven years in Manhattan had been awesome, but at my core I was not a city kid. The idea of working and living in Greenwich appealed to me greatly—as did Ted's performance- driven compensation plan.

I arrived at Greenwich Capital as a pretty decent young salesman and three years later, through hard work and osmosis, I had gotten better. Ted noticed my progress and asked me to have a hamburger with him. At dinner, to my astonishment, Ted opened the conversation by saying, "*I want you to know that I believe you will someday be the CEO of Greenwich Capital.*" I don't remember if I said anything in reply, but most likely I was too surprised to say anything. Ted didn't go into any detail about why he had singled me out, and I didn't ask him because I was afraid too much examination of the issue might lead him to a different conclusion. However, Ted did say I would need to get some experience trading and I readily agreed to that stipulation. I went home and told Leigh the good news, called my mother and told her the good news, and gave my two-year-old daughter, Avery, a big hug. I could not believe my good fortune. I was on Cloud Nine!

Unfortunately, for the next two years, I proved myself to be an exceptionally untalented trader (I consistently lost money). I came to understand selling was like sports: The harder you work the more successful you become. However, trading is much tougher because you are competing against the market—which is the aggregate of everyone's knowledge.

After those two years it was obvious to Ted, and to my direct boss Gary Holloway, I should not continue trading. I assume they were also seriously reconsidering their career plans for me. All was not wrong with the world, however, because in August 1992 my second daughter, Kendall, was born. I was now the proud father of two beautiful girls—I just needed to get my career back on track. Against that backdrop, two months after Kendall was born, a new concern suddenly appeared on stage and commanded the spotlight.

Getting Lucky

On October 20, 1992, I was sitting at my desk (probably trying to figure out how to stop losing money trading) when it felt like my chest exploded! This is no exaggeration. One minute I was fine and the next I could barely walk or talk and was in excruciating agony. I asked my good friend, Morris Sachs (who was one of the firm's star traders and whose desk was next to mine), to take me to Greenwich Hospital and I staggered out to his car.

When we got to the hospital, I was in bad shape. The pain was so intense I hoped I would pass out. But until the doctors figured out what was wrong they weren't going to give me any painkillers which would mask the symptoms. I lay on a table in the ER in agony and, like the doctors outside my room, wondered what was going on.

Morris called Leigh and soon she was by my side. I wanted to put on a brave face, but the pain was too intense. After Leigh was with me for a few minutes, I turned to her and said, "*I don't know what is going to happen, but I want you to know how much I love you and the girls.*" Being the daughter of a surgeon, Leigh has always had a deep-seated reverence for doctors; however, hearing her husband, in essence, say goodbye was as if a starter gun went off. Without saying a word, Leigh flew out the door into the hall where the doctors were attending to a variety of patients while they tried to decide what to do with me. Then I heard Leigh, not hysterically but *very* firmly and loudly, say to the doctors, "*My husband is DYING and he needs all your attention RIGHT NOW!*"

Immediately, all three ER doctors were in my room and, after a few quick tests were administered, they decided my problem couldn't be handled at Greenwich Hospital. The last thing I remember was being strapped to a stretcher by the medical helicopter paramedics who were airlifting me to Yale-New Haven Hospital.

That night at the hospital was not a good one for Leigh, her parents, or my parents. The doctors prepared everyone for the worst. The issue was whether I had gotten to the hospital in time, or if too much internal damage had already been done to save me. Afterwards, my surgeon was emphatic that if I had arrived at Yale-New Haven even a few minutes later it would have been all over.

A few days later my college roommate, John Small, had his father (who was a surgeon) call Leigh's father (who was also a surgeon). After that conversation Dr. Small told John, "*Ben will probably live, but don't expect him to be the same person you knew before.*" When I regained consciousness three days later, I didn't know what day it was. Leigh, who I later learned was at my bedside the entire time, was there. I had a breathing tube down my throat, so I couldn't talk. I made a writing gesture and a nurse brought me a pencil and a note pad. I remember scratching out two words—"*what happened?*"—and giving it to Leigh.

What happened was I suffered an aortic dissection. Most people who experience this kind of dissection die immediately from internal bleeding because the aorta is the artery all your blood travels through before being distributed to the rest of your body. Much later, I came to understand I had a rare genetic disorder called Marfan's (which affects one out of every 5,000 people) that caused this dissection. After three weeks, I was out of the ICU and into a step-down care unit at the hospital.

While still in a good deal of pain, I was starting to feel pretty lucky. I hadn't died and I was starting to look forward to getting on with my life. I felt like I had been hit by a random bullet, had lived to tell the tale, and was going to be just fine. That is until my surgeon, Dr. Letsou, came by to see me one evening while Leigh and her parents were in my room.

Dr. Letsou explained that while I was extremely fortunate to have survived my dissection, I was far from just fine. The dissection, which started just above my heart, had severely damaged my entire aorta (which runs from the heart to the lower pelvis). He explained the aorta is the central pressure point for the human body. Each heartbeat shoots blood out of the heart into the aorta with great velocity. To withstand the pressure, the aorta is constructed like three concentric garden hoses. The medical term for these hoses are walls. During my dissection, the inner wall broke and blood forced its way between the inner and middle wall which tore the inner wall to shreds from the top of my heart down through my chest and abdomen. Next, blood began leaking into my heart sac, which is the area surrounding the heart, that needs to be unobstructed to allow the heart to contract and expand properly. With each beat, as my heart contracted, more blood entered the heart sac and began choking my heart because now there was not enough space for the heart to expand back into. Dr. Letsou explained he had, just barely, been able to patch my aorta before my blood choked my heart to death. However, he had not even attempted to deal with the damage to the rest of my aorta.

Dr. Letsou concluded by saying I would need many more major surgeries in the future (he was right—I have now had seven) and I could *never* run or lift anything heavy for the rest of my life. To say I was devastated would be a gross understatement. I loved competitive sports and, maybe most importantly, my self-image had always been closely tied to confidence in myself physically. Now that was gone—forever.

Lying in my hospital bed, a kind of blackness I never knew existed enveloped me. Trying to keep it together, I choked out a "*thank you*" to Dr. Letsou and asked Leigh and her parents to go out to dinner. Understanding me better than anyone, Leigh quickly kissed me goodbye and left with her parents. I was alone and for a few minutes I don't think I moved a muscle. My mind raced around in circles but went nowhere. I was lost in the blackness. What happened next is still a mystery to me. I don't know where they came from, but suddenly four words entered my consciousness: "*Everything Will Be Okay.*"

That was all I needed. As quickly as the blackness had come—it was gone. Despite having been dragged to church as a child by my mother, formal religion had never meant much to me, but I believe the appearance of those four words was the one truly spiritual moment in my life. I don't believe I had the mental strength to accept that news the way I did without some "outside help." Whatever the reason, when Leigh and her parents returned from dinner, I was a new man. Everything *was* going to be okay and, while the game may have changed, I was still going to enjoy playing. My brush with "outside help" is something I will never forget. However, the real lesson from my health scare is to understand if you were granted just one wish, you should wish for a partner who is smart, loves you, and will look out for you.

Almost Killing My Boss

Despite dealing well with my health situation, I knew my once promising career was in serious jeopardy and I had a wife and two tiny daughters depending on me. I no longer felt like the CEO in waiting, but very much as I had during most of my childhood—a little overwhelmed, but determined to succeed. From the hospital I called Gary Holloway and told him I wanted to go back to what I was good at—selling bonds. Gary's response surprised me when he said he understood and he offered me the job as sales manager for U.S. Treasuries—which was a huge promotion.

After I got out of the hospital, I repaid Gary for his loyalty and faith in me by almost killing him. It was mid-December and my first appearance at Greenwich Capital was at our annual holiday party. In a very Ted-like twist, our firm was hyper-casual, but our holiday party was hyper-formal—suits and ties for the men and evening dresses for the women. That year it was held at a fancy private club with, as always, an elaborate sit-down dinner. Being just back from the dead, I was the unofficial guest of honor and placed at Gary's table—right next to the man himself.

After everyone was seated, Gary put his arm around me and asked how I was feeling. It was obvious to all I was not doing so well. I could barely walk upright and, while always thin, I now looked emaciated. At that moment, I sensed Gary's question was only partly based on humanitarian concerns. Now that he was seeing my severely weakened condition, it also belied a professional concern about whether I would be able to handle the demanding job of sales manager for the firm's flagship business.

With no premeditation, I looked Gary straight in the eyes and said, "*I'm doing great…but I just can't seem to remember anything.*" With my declaration of mental incompetence, I saw all the blood drain from his face. I resumed eating as if I just commented on the weather and allowed Gary to contemplate, for a moment, the situation he was now facing with his newly appointed, brain-addled, sales manager. After a few bites I looked at Gary, smiled, and told him I was kidding. To his credit, Gary was *much* more relieved than angry and he seemed to take the joke as a sign that, despite my obvious physical frailty, I was my old self again.

LEARNING FROM A SLUMP

Having Gary promote me to be the sales manager for Treasury bonds was probably the most surprising thing that happened in my career.

My previous two years at Greenwich Capital had been positively insane. They started with the incredible high of Ted telling me someday I would run the firm, followed by the devastating low of failing as a trader, and then I nearly died. After all that, while I was still in the hospital (with no visitors except family allowed), Gary made me the U.S. Treasury sales manager. Why was he entrusting this critical job to me at this time?

About a year into my trading career, my failure to make money began to eat away at me. I no longer felt like a rookie trader still learning the ropes. I now felt like a full blown failure and found myself slipping into a shell. I kept thinking, *"If I can't make money trading, what possible contributions can I make to the trading floor which is all about making money?"* This was the first real failure I experienced in my career and it felt as if my nightmare bogeyman, who I thought was successfully locked away in the past, had broken free and was rapidly gaining on me. After a few months of feeling beaten down, I finally got a grip and consciously forced myself to keep moving around the floor, encouraging and congratulating others, even as I was personally failing—but it was tough. I believe my background as an athlete helped—just because your batting average is poor doesn't mean you withdraw and stop being a good teammate.

As every veteran slumping hitter will tell you, he needs to keep working harder at batting practice, but he doesn't want to focus too much on getting hits because that can be counterproductive. I could not control my poor trading, but I could control how I responded to it. I worked harder learning how to trade and, as importantly, made certain my struggles did not bring down the team or my teammates' perception of me. Even now, thinking about that time in my career makes me feel ill. It's scary and no fun being in a long deep slump.

You are going to experience good and bad times. It is during the bad times you need to draw on all the strength you can muster to stay focused

on your goals and keep moving forward. The word for this is resilience
and you must be resilient in order to sustain your effort and determi-
nation to succeed. I believe it was the resilience I showed while failing
that made Gary want to promote me at a time of grave crisis for both my
health and career.

BACK ON TRACK

Though I did a good job of not letting my failure as a trader (or the
failure of my aorta) bury me emotionally, both experiences took a
toll and it felt great to return to sales. While I always enjoyed the
sales and trading business, and always loved working at Greenwich
Capital, I had a renewed appreciation for both.

The Cowboy

There were many similarities between Ted and The Cowboy. They
were roughly the same size and age, they were both great athletes
and leaders, and they both loved to have a good time. The Cowboy,
however, had a much harder edge. That was probably a good thing
because, as the head of trading at Greenwich Capital, he had a tough
job: managing all the traders as well as his own trading account.
I remember Ted once saying to me, "*It's great to have The Cowboy*
around because he gives everyone else courage."

Hiring The Cowboy was a huge coup for Greenwich Capital
and a testament to what a great recruiter Ted was. Prior to joining
Greenwich, The Cowboy worked as a trader in John Meriwether's
legendary proprietary trading group at Solomon Brothers. In the
1980s, Solomon was the undisputed king of the fixed income
trading jungle and Meriwether's traders were the biggest and
baddest (i.e., most profitable) apes in that jungle. For a highly
regarded trader to leave Meriwether's team and join a small upstart
firm was quite surprising, but great salesmen like Ted often generate

surprising outcomes. The Cowboy didn't disappoint, and during his time at Greenwich he skillfully and successfully managed the firm's traders and risk.

In his mid 40s, after seven years at Greenwich Capital, The Cowboy retired from the business and moved to Steamboat Springs to raise his family, ski, fly his plane, and trade the money he made during his Wall Street career. When I moved back into sales in 1993, The Cowboy had just left Greenwich and he became one of my clients. The Cowboy was better known for his quick draw wit than for warm words of praise or encouragement. I enjoyed covering The Cowboy because he was very smart and I appreciated his rough brand of humor which, along with bonds, we traded back and forth.

After covering The Cowboy for a couple of years, one day we were discussing Greenwich Capital and I said something positive about the firm. Rather than ripping me with a wisecrack, The Cowboy said, "*You know, I think you should run Greenwich Capital someday.*" I mumbled something like, "*That would be nice,*" but he wouldn't let it go. He said, "*I'm serious, you are the most enthusiastic person at Greenwich about Greenwich and that's what it takes.*" Though I was surprised when Ted first broached this topic, I was even more surprised by The Cowboy's comment. That's because, unlike Ted, The Cowboy was quite reserved when it came to compliments.

It is also important to note what The Cowboy didn't say. He didn't say I was the smartest, hardest working, or most organized person. He only said I was the most enthusiastic, but to The Cowboy that's what mattered most.

KEEP YOUR EYES ON THE PRIZE

By 1994, I had been at Greenwich Capital for eight years, had been a sales manager for two, and I was very happy in my current job. For instance, when The Cowboy mentioned the idea of me becoming the CEO, I hadn't given it much thought. This is because the current Co-CEOs, Gary and his partner, Chip Kruger, were doing a great job and, more importantly, within my department there were two guys ahead of me. Both were well-liked, highly successful traders, and very good friends of mine. In effect, the three of us acted as partners running the U.S. Treasury bond business—with me as the junior partner. I will call the first trader The Prince (both for his position and because he was a highly "principled" guy) and the second trader The King (because he *was* The King!).

The Prince

The Prince was a Harvard graduate with Midwestern good looks, and he was a great athlete with an outgoing personality. He was about my age and had joined Greenwich Capital three years before I arrived. He ran the trading desk while I was the sales manager.

The Prince was quirky—but in an endearing way. At one point he felt, due to stress and business travel, he was neglecting his family. So, The Prince invited his wife and two young children to have lunch with him at work—which was unusual but certainly a nice idea. What amazed everyone was when The Prince spread out a blanket on the floor next to his desk, in the middle of an extremely busy trading floor with traders and salespeople shouting all around. The Prince and his family sat there and, to all appearances, had as pleasant and genteel a picnic lunch as if they spread their blanket on the mountain meadow from which Julie Andrews sang in the opening scene of *The Sound of Music*.

So what happened to The Prince? Well, in 1994, he had a terrific year trading and was going to be one of the highest—possibly *the* highest—compensated Treasury bond trader on all of Wall Street. But there was a problem. The Prince, like most Greenwich Capital traders, was on Ted's performance-driven compensation plan which meant his pay was formulaic. However, The Prince had a disagreement with his boss, The King, about how part of his formula should be calculated. The dispute was over a good deal of money—but it was still only 10% of the Prince's total compensation for the year. Because I was so close to the situation, I can tell you this was a legitimate disagreement over a reasonably technical issue. Eventually, Gary stepped in and paid The Prince the disputed monies to keep him happy. That should have been the end of it, but it wasn't. The Prince, feeling he had been *disrespected* by The King, resigned from Greenwich Capital. I begged The Prince to stay, both because we were friends and because of his tremendous trading talents, but he wouldn't relent. As I said, he was *very* principled.

I didn't understand how The Prince could allow such a dispute to so negatively influence his career. Shockingly—I assumed because he couldn't find a firm as fun or as lucrative as Greenwich Capital—The Prince never worked as a trader again. Well, although I wasn't happy about it, that was one down.

The King

Now it was just The King and I. The King had it all wired. He had gone to college with Ted, was one of the first employees hired by him in the early days of Greenwich Capital and, like The Prince, he was a highly talented and profitable trader. The King was also a workout fiend and 6′6″ of tempered steel. He was assumed by everyone, including me, to be a lock to take the top job when it became available—but it was not to be.

Why? Because The King was every bit as quirky as The Prince—only in different ways. The King operated on his own timetable. He thought quickly and moved slowly. For a few years I sat next to The King and I marveled at the way he ate his food. A single three-inch potato chip would take him a solid two minutes to consume as he would take tiny bites with his front teeth and chew it until, I assume, it vaporized in his mouth. While pretty strange, The King's style of eating didn't negatively impact others, but his inability to abide by a schedule did.

When I got to the firm, The King was already legendary for being late. It was called "King Time" which meant if you were scheduled to meet him for dinner you should expect The King to be *two hours late*. I'm not kidding...two hours was typical, and three hours was not unheard of! Before The King became a manager, most of his dinners were with Wall Street brokers who made commissions if The King traded with them. They would have happily waited a month for The King to arrive. The King was making lots of money for Greenwich Capital and, when The King finally did arrive, he was always great fun to be with.

All was good in the kingdom until The King started to climb the corporate ladder. Ultimately, the firm's entire U.S. Treasury business reported to him. *Now* there were *plenty* of problems. King Time no longer worked when he was on top with more than 200 people depending on him. The King had to be taken out of the running to become CEO because he simply could not get anywhere on time. So who was left from the Treasury side? You guessed it, me.

While The Prince and The King were unique characters, any person who ascends the ladder of a large organization has his own stories about the people who were ahead of him and why they left, failed, or chose not to compete. Someone has to get the top job and it is almost never solely because that individual is so much better than everyone else. This is another good reason to keep a healthy dose of humility at the top of the ladder.

OUT ON A LIMB

Consistent with Ted's philosophy that execution mattered more than strategy—there were few strategy meetings at Greenwich

Capital. Despite that corporate bias and history, towards the end of 1995, the Co-CEO's of Greenwich Capital, Chip and Gary, decided to hold a firm-wide year-end review of all businesses—complete with plans for 1996 and beyond. While hardly a radical idea for a growing company with multiple product lines, it was new to us. In the past, all firm-wide events had two goals: The first was to bring all employees together and have a good time, and the second was to celebrate the firm's continued success.

Though this event was held at a nice venue on the water, just down the road from our offices, it was all business. With a few hundred in attendance, each department ran through their results and plans for the new year. Not surprisingly, the presentations were heavy on budgets and numbers. When it was my turn, I dutifully ran through the numbers for my business, but I went off script, and out on a limb, when I concluded my presentation by saying, "*While our competitors are all much larger, and have the advantage of providing our clients many more products, I believe we have the talent to become the #1 U.S. Treasury Primary Dealership in the world. It will take a lot of hard work, and our competitors will fight us tooth and nail, but we can do this.*"

In my eight years at Greenwich, I had never heard anyone make such a statement. We were proud of our success, but the firm still viewed itself as "the little engine that could" and not as a market leader. I believe this was partly because of the enormous size of our competitors, but also because of our founder and North Star, Ted. Being such a people person, Ted thought about most issues in terms of individual, not firm, achievements. While that was the genius of Ted, and a big reason for Greenwich Capital's early success, I believed the company was at an inflection point and it was time for the entire firm, and not just individuals, to aspire to greatness.

Going out on a limb and publicly declaring my ambitions for my department probably affected me more than anyone else. I began to regularly say to myself, "*We can do this,*" as I contemplated Greenwich Capital's path to become a market leader.

As we continued to hire experienced "A" players from our competitors, the building blocks for the foundation of that dream started to fall into place. Because of our outstanding traders, salespeople, strategists, economists, and support, our share of our customers' business began to rise sharply. Profits followed suit, and both our U.S. Treasury Primary Dealership and our Mortgage and Asset Backed Department began to generate an increased amount of attention from both clients and competitors.

A few months after the big strategy meeting, on April Fool's Day 1996, Leigh's and my family became complete with the arrival of our third daughter, Cameron. Suddenly, it seemed the stars had aligned for my personal and professional life. However, as is so often the case, that's when the next challenge rises up.

CUT THROAT AND DEEP THROAT

In 1999, seven years after my first surgery, my health again became a major issue. I had three major aortic surgeries that year. Literally, as I was getting back on my feet from one operation, I was being knocked down by the next. The last one, as collateral damage, cut one of my vocal cords so I could barely speak. For all of that year I did most of my work, and held most of my meetings, lying on the sofa in my office.

In addition to my personal physical crisis, the year had been a wild ride for Greenwich Capital. For some time, institutional investors who owned the majority of the equity of our parent company, NatWest, had been dissatisfied with the performance of the bank and they were open to the idea of NatWest being bought by another company. To get these institutional investors to support their bid to buy NatWest, the Royal Bank of Scotland came up with a strategic plan outlining what they would do with NatWest following the purchase. Despite knowing little about Greenwich Capital, RBS decided it would sound good to investors to announce they were going to concentrate only on core businesses—and a bond trading firm headquartered in the USA, which operated autonomously, did not qualify as core.

One day in early January 2000, while I lay on my office sofa, Ted walked in, closed the door behind him and sat down at my desk. I could tell he had something serious to discuss. With none of his customary lighthearted small talk he said, "*Mr. Ben, do you know Chip and Gary are planning to leave once this deal with RBS goes through?*" In my barely audible whisper, I told Ted I had heard that. Ted then asked, "*Do you still want to be CEO of this company?*" While Ted and I had become good friends, surprisingly, we had never spoken again about me becoming CEO since that hamburger dinner he bought me 10 years before. I think that was because the position of CEO hadn't become available during that time and, just as importantly, I had my hands full trying to stay alive and do my job. However, with the top job now up for grabs, I told Ted that I "*absolutely*" still wanted it. Then Ted, like Watergate's Deep Throat, cryptically gave me a tiny scrap of hugely important classified information. He said, "*There are people in this company who don't think you can handle the job physically, and if you want to be CEO you have to fight for it—right now.*" With that, Ted stood up, wished me luck, and walked out of my office less than a minute after he entered.

As Ted closed the door behind him, I tried to assimilate what he said. The good news was great: Ted was in my corner. The bad news was some others weren't. Given the abysmal state of my health for the past year, looking at it objectively, I don't think I would have thought it was a good idea for me to become the CEO. But I wasn't objective and I wanted the job. Ted hadn't divulged who was concerned about my health, but I knew the opinions of only three guys mattered: Ted, Chip, and Gary. Already having Ted's support, all I needed was one more vote and since I reported directly to Gary it was clear it needed to be his.

I had worked for Gary my entire 13-year career at Greenwich Capital and we were always very friendly, but never close. This had nothing to do with Gary's personality; he was someone I would have been proud to have as a good friend. Given our professional relationship, however, I don't think either of us wanted to become too close because in business it is generally a good thing to have a certain amount of personal distance between people who directly report to one another. However, I firmly believed Gary would support me if he could be convinced it wouldn't be detrimental to my health.

There was only one person in the world who could speak with authority on the issue of my health, and that was my surgeon, Len Girardi, at New York Hospital. Len grew up outside Pittsburgh and was the first in his family to attend college. He went to Harvard as an undergraduate, played football there, and went on to medical school at Cornell. Despite being only 39 years old, Len was already one of a handful of world-renowned vascular surgeons and he kept busy. He did more than 500 surgeries a year with the vast majority being the delicate, lengthy and highly specialized, life-critical aortic surgeries he performed on me. In the medical community, he was a top gun fighter pilot and if you had my medical issues you didn't want anyone but him flying missions for you. I slowly and gingerly made my way from the sofa to my desk and called Len. Miraculously, I got him on the phone:

Me (whispering weakly): *Hi Len, how's everything?*

Len (sounding busy): *Pretty good Ben—what's up?*

Me (sounding worried): *There's some stuff going on here at work and there's a chance I could become CEO if I can handle the job physically…what do you think?*

Len (asking a question I hadn't anticipated): *Will you have to do any heavy lifting or running?*

Me (liking where this was going): *No.*

Len (again sounding pretty busy): *You'll be fine.*

Me (sounding relieved and hopeful): *Would you be willing to talk to my boss and tell him that?*

Len (with his voice now getting gradually weaker as, I assume, he was in the act of hanging up to do something more important than talk to Ben about his career): *Sure, have him call me.* (click)

The next day I arranged for Gary and Len to speak on the phone. First, Len addressed why I looked, and felt, so God-awful after these aortic replacement surgeries. Len explained this was the most painful of all surgeries because of the huge area covered by the aorta and how difficult it was to get to.

Len further told Gary my heart was in good shape and my health issues were all related to my rare connective tissue disorder. Finally, Len explained that concerns about stress in the workplace, leading to health problems, were widely misunderstood. For example, most people believe that, by itself, stress is harmful to your heart. However, the heart and aorta are not organs capably of rational thought—that job is reserved for the brain. In a case such as mine, Len opined that stress can actually be a good thing because it gets you out of bed in the morning with a sense of purpose—which *is* good for your mental and physical health. Since I had no history of high blood pressure, Len assured Gary that even if I experienced stress from work, it was likely my aorta would remain blissfully ignorant and unaffected.

Throughout the call, Gary peppered Len with tough questions about the prospects for my health over both the short and long term. Len, genuinely believing what he was saying, but also understanding how much I wanted this job, batted all these questions away like an

NHL goalie. Finally, Gary took one last hard shot: "*So, you're telling me Ben can be the CEO of this company?*" Len responded with the precision of a surgeon and perhaps a dose of levity, "*I can't tell you Ben should be the CEO, but I can tell you I don't believe the job will kill him.*" The coast was clear.

GOING TO WAR

Before Ted's Deep Throat conversation with me, in the immediate aftermath of RBS winning approval to purchase NatWest, Chip and Gary were the only Greenwich Capital employees to have substantive discussions with RBS about our company. Nothing they heard gave them confidence that RBS would allow Greenwich to continue to operate autonomously. Soon after, Chip and Gary resigned from Greenwich and Ted also announced his departure. Things were not looking good and Greenwich Capital employees were getting more uncertain and worried by the minute. Despite sharing the concerns of other employees, I realized there was some very good news for me. Not only did I get named Co-CEO of Greenwich Capital, but my partner, Jay Levine, was a great guy from the mortgage side of the business.

Jay had come to Greenwich eight years earlier (from Solomon Brothers) and he had the mortgage business in his blood. He grew up in California and his father had founded and owned a successful mortgage origination company. Jay was smart, hard-working, and he loved the business. Also, he wholeheartedly subscribed to Ted's belief that business and fun went hand in hand. But before Greenwich Capital could get back to having fun, there was one specific task that needed to be accomplished. Jay and I understood a people business could not perform well if employees were distracted or, worse, frightened. Our #1 mission was to take charge in a decisive way by clearly communicating a simple message and plan.

The Meeting

In our first act as Co-CEOs, Jay and I called a meeting of the entire firm in the cafeteria and delivered this message to employees:

> We can't let ourselves be distracted by what is going on in the markets or what is going on at RBS. We don't control the markets or RBS, but we do control how we respond to these challenges.
>
> Who cares if RBS ultimately sells us or keeps us? If we continue to perform well, there are many companies who would love to acquire Greenwich Capital and we will be able to dictate terms.
>
> However, if we allow ourselves to be distracted and our performance suffers, no one will want us and even if we eventually do find a home we will lose the autonomy and culture that we treasure and is the key to our success.
>
> We need to do this for the sake of our firm, our careers, and our families who are depending on us!

Soon after our meeting with employees, Jay and I met with the senior management of RBS who decided to visit Greenwich one time before they made a final decision about what to do with these "non-core" Americans. Feeling the cards were stacked against us, Jay and I decided to get aggressive and we gave an impassioned sales pitch about the strengths of Greenwich Capital and, most importantly, what we saw as the potential for our company going forward. It felt as if we were playing high-stakes poker, on behalf of 550 employees and their families, with only a small stack of chips in front of us—which we pushed "all in" to the pot.

Jay and I left that meeting with no idea of what to expect. However, a few weeks later we received better news than we ever dreamt when RBS made a public announcement reversing their decision to sell Greenwich Capital. In that press release, RBS stated it intended to "ring-fence" the firm (i.e., continue to let us operate autonomously) while they concentrated on integrating NatWest into RBS. At that point, Jay and I met with Ted and asked him to return to Greenwich Capital as a spiritual leader. Ted, who clearly wasn't ready for the fun to end, gave us both a huge hug and said, "*Hell Yes!*"

For Greenwich Capital employees, having RBS publicly and loudly proclaim they intended to sell the firm had been like a cavalry of 550 soldiers being thrown off their horses at the same time. Employees felt bruised and scared. However, as Jay and I continued to proselytize our message of salvation through performance, Ted announced he was staying, and RBS announced it was ring-fencing Greenwich Capital—those 550 people got back up on their horses, the horses broke into a full gallop, and no one slowed down for the next seven years!

The Results

The decision to keep Greenwich Capital proved to be an outstanding one for both RBS and Greenwich Capital. In the early 2000s, Greenwich Capital's two primary business lines really hit their stride. First the U.S. Treasury Dealership, and then the Mortgage and Asset Backed Department, began being perennially ranked #1 in the world by the largest 100 institutional clients globally.*

The quality of our client relationships, combined with our talented traders, paved the way for our firm's financial performance. From 1999 to 2006, Greenwich Capital increased its pre-tax profit 500%. In 2006, our firm generated $1.25 billion in pre-tax profit with only 1,250 employees—which is $1 million of pre-tax profit per employee. As I was stepping down from an operating role at the beginning of 2007, I was curious how the performance of Greenwich Capital stacked up against our competitors. I used Goldman Sachs as a comparison because they were historically the most profitable and highly regarded Wall Street firm. When I looked at the

---

*According to the independent consulting firm Orion Consultants.

results for the time Jay and I were CO-CEOs, even I was startled. From 2000 to 2006, Greenwich Capital averaged $796,000 pre-tax profit per employee, versus $288,000 for Goldman Sachs. This means, for those seven years, Greenwich Capital was nearly three times more profitable per head than the most prestigious firm on Wall Street.*

LOOKING BACK

Part One of *The Bigs* is titled "How to Survive, Thrive, and Have Fun in the Big Leagues," and not "How To Become a Corporate CEO," for two reasons. First, as you now know, the process of becoming a CEO in a large organization is fraught with events you can't control. Second, this book is about the journey and *not* the destination. Statistically, only a tiny percentage of employees in a large organization can become the CEO. However, in those same large organizations, a considerable percentage of employees will have jobs and careers they enjoy and find rewarding.

While I certainly did enjoy being the Co-CEO of Greenwich Capital, the most fun I had in my career was being a sales manager. Working on the trading floor, surrounded by my friends, knee-deep in the markets, selling, managing, and recruiting was a perfect fit for me. Also, this was easily the hardest I worked during my entire Wall Street career. I came home every night exhausted—but I couldn't wait to get up in the morning and do it again.

If you are going to pursue a corporate career, my advice is to strive to find a job that fits your talents, interests, and skills the way being a sales manager did for me. (And, *The Bigs* is here to help

---

*The other investment bank which was a reasonable comparison to Greenwich Capital was my old employer, Morgan Stanley. From 2000–2006, Morgan Stanley averaged $126,961 of pre-tax profit per head. By that metric, Greenwich Capital was almost eight times more profitable than Morgan Stanley.

you do just that!) The perfect fit industry and company will be different for everyone. However, if you are determined enough, you *will* find a situation that allows you to have fun, create substantial value to your company, and get paid fairly for your contributions.

If becoming a CEO is your goal, the only way to get there is by doing your very best at every rung on the ladder (even if you, like me, sometimes fail). If you catch the right breaks and achieve your ultimate goal—great. If not, you will still have enjoyed a highly successful career.

GOING FORWARD

When I stepped down from being Co-CEO of Greenwich Capital at the beginning of 2007, I was leaving my dream job. People have often said I was a genius to foresee the impending financial crisis and get out of the way, however, I was not that smart. All I knew was that after 26 years in the business, five major surgeries, and having achieved the goals I set for myself and the firm, it was time for a change. I remember the moment, in the spring of 2006, when I realized this. I had gone out for a walk, something I never would have done in the old days, and I didn't want to go back to the office. That sounds pretty benign, but I always *loved* being at Greenwich Capital and I realized this was the proverbial canary in the mineshaft. In March of 2007, I officially stepped down from the Co-CEO role, resigned from the board, and became a vice chairman of the firm, which was a ceremonial title. Happily, in doing so, I was able to move my office downstairs next to the other vice chairman—my good friend Ted.

Another issue was, starting in 2006, RBS began to dismantle the ring-fence and integrate our firm into their global banking business. The autonomy Greenwich Capital always enjoyed was the foundation on which the firm built its unique culture. That culture was the reason top professionals were attracted to Greenwich, why few ever left, and why the firm became so outrageously successful. In April 2009, RBS symbolically completed the integration by officially retiring the Greenwich Capital brand name. I still cared a great deal about many of my former colleagues who remained at RBS, but the name change extinguished any lingering allegiance I felt to that special firm Ted started 28 years earlier—it was gone. Feeling similarly, Ted also officially left the firm around this time. Fortunately, this sad occasion coincided with an exciting new business opportunity.

Let's Do It Again

Two months later, in June 2009, Jay Levine (my Greenwich Capital Co-CEO partner), Ron Kripalani (a talented and highly regarded Wall Street veteran), Bob Eick (a charismatic and standout salesman from Greenwich Capital), and I decided to buy CRT Capital. CRT was a 20-year-old broker-dealer that was struggling and Jay, Ron, Bob, and I thought it would be fun to try to recreate some of the magic of Greenwich Capital. Now, four years in, and using Ted's playbook, we have hired many former Greenwich Capital professionals as well as many top professionals from other Wall Street firms. We also successfully recapitalized CRT with an equity raise led by Aquiline Capital Partners. CRT's headcount has increased from 100 to 300 employees and I believe we are on our way!

FINAL THOUGHTS

In the next chapter we dive into the exciting world of entrepreneurship. However, before we move on, it is important for you to appreciate the benefits that come from beginning, and perhaps staying, in a corporate career. The following are just some of the highly valuable benefits I enjoyed while working at Bankers Trust, Morgan Stanley, and Greenwich Capital:

- The opportunity to work with, and learn from, many talented professionals and co-workers.

- The opportunity to establish a network of professional contacts, starting with your co-workers. Over time, it is likely your co-workers will migrate to other companies and your network of contacts will expand. These contacts can be invaluable sources of business opportunities, helpful if you want to switch jobs, or pools of talent to hire from when you get into a leadership position.

- The "leverage" of working at a big company. A big company has big resources and, if you do a great job, ultimately you will be given access to those resources. With your talent and those resources, you have the opportunity to make a lot money for the company and yourself.

- The financial security of working for a company that is likely (but not guaranteed) to be around tomorrow.

- The ability to learn the business and make mistakes that will not "sink the ship."

Chapter 2

Being an Entrepreneur

As you now know, my primary career was not as an entrepreneur. However, you also know how close I came to chucking my corporate career to try my hand as an entrepreneur and nightclub impresario. While I had a great time working in the sales and trading business, my real passion has always been start-ups. Well before ever hanging an "Open for Business" sign, I love coming up with entrepreneurial ideas and researching these ideas. What I most enjoy is talking to people involved in the industry and then deciding which of their ideas I will incorporate into my plan. In fact, I am so interested in new business ventures, I believe it took an unusual company and opportunity in the corporate world (Greenwich Capital) to keep me in that world for my primary career.

One reason I find start-ups so compelling is every significant decision made in a small company is a matter of life or death for that enterprise. In business, simplicity is good and complexity is bad. Many lessons are best taught by looking at small companies since they are, by definition, less complex. However, all businesses, large and small, share much more in common than most people appreciate. After all, a large company is nothing more than a small company that grew, and we all know the fundamental DNA of anything does not change with growth—it just gets bigger.

There are no bright lines between what constitutes an entrepreneurial and a corporate company. A perfect example is Greenwich Capital that began life as a classic entrepreneurial start-up and over time became more corporate. This is the life cycle of many highly successful companies. Entrepreneurial and corporate jobs each have their own strengths and challenges. I will start by sharing a few examples of entrepreneurial projects I have been involved with and describe what made some winners and some losers. I have had too many entrepreneurial ideas to delve into all of them. However, I believe these four are worth examination: Tumble Inn, All Cotton, Golfone, and The Stand. They were all obsessions of mine at one time and there are important lessons to be learned from each of them.

TUMBLE INN

My most successful early entrepreneurial idea came to me in 1981. I was less than a year out of college and was working at Bankers Trust in Manhattan. I was invited by a friend, Ebby Gerry, to play on a softball team sponsored by Murphy's (an old Upper East Side Irish bar that attracted a rabid following of young professionals). I had never spent much time at Murphy's, but as a member of the softball team I was now there twice a week for more hours than I could count.

Murphy's was a gold mine. Packed every night with young professionals who had money to burn (no children yet) and who all seemed to have an unquenchable thirst for beer. What amazed me most, however, was not that the bar was so successful, but how little the bar owner seemed to have done to generate this loyal following. Even the softball team was Ebby's idea and he had to beg the bar to sponsor us. One night, with the typical Murphy's pandemonium going on around me, I had a thought: "*I could do this!*" All I needed was to find a struggling bar in the same general area and strike a deal with the owner. The next day after work, I explained the idea to my girlfriend, Leigh. She humored me and said the idea sounded "interesting," probably hoping that would be the end of it. Well, not quite!

That night, after a day spent writing credit reports for Bankers Trust, I traded in my suit and tie for a T-shirt, jeans, and sneakers, and headed out into the neighborhood between my apartment, at 94th and Third Avenue, and Murphy's at 87th and First Avenue. This was the hottest neighborhood for college grads fresh out of school. My newly opened apartment building was a perfect example, being stuffed full of 1980 college graduates, reaching 30 stories into the sky.

It would be fun to regale you with stories of the bars I went into, the owners I talked to, and how, after an exhaustive search, I finally found the perfect spot. The only problem is that's not what happened. What did happen is, after a pleasant stroll around the neighborhood, I found myself two blocks north of Murphy's, standing outside a bar I had never seen, or at least never noticed before. This bar had a small, crudely painted, chipped, and faded name on the front window: "Tumble Inn."

Before crossing the threshold of idea to action, I stepped back and looked the building over carefully. It was at the corner of 89th and First Avenue, a single-story building with two small windows and a door which opened onto First Avenue. The longer side, on 89th Street, was windowless, covered in plywood, and tagged with graffiti. The Tumble Inn was the most beat up, run down, and forlorn looking bar I had ever seen on the East Side and it didn't get any better when I opened the door.

Except for two neon beer signs glowing dimly, it looked like nothing but abuse had been visited upon the Tumble Inn since the Great Depression. The layout of the bar was fine: a single rectangular space, the length of a bowling alley and half that width, with a bar covered in peeling laminate wood running down the entire right side. The only furnishings were a few bar stools, two tables, eight chairs, and a pool table—all of which were obviously of poor quality when they were purchased and were now disintegrating. The only aspect of the space that could conceivably been called gracious was the height of the ceiling which was 10′ throughout.

When I entered the Tumble Inn, not only did the physical plant look like a movie set for a Depression-era movie, but the three people in the bar—two old men slumping on bar stools and a slightly younger white-haired woman behind the bar—looked like they had been cast for an urban sequel to *The Grapes of Wrath*. Time and grime had conspired to turn everything a dark gray. I walked in, sat down between the two old guys, ordered a beer, and started talking to the bartender, whom I soon came to understand was the owner of this august establishment.

Margie

With her snow-white hair and strong personality, Margie provided the only color in the bar. She was in her late 50s and maybe five feet tall. She had been a bartender at the Tumble Inn for most of her working life and took over the bar from the previous owner years ago. Margie grew up in the neighborhood, had a classic New York in-your-face personality, and the accent to go with it. After we got to know each other, she would preface all verbal communication to me by first barking rapidly "*Ben Ben Ben*"…and then telling me whatever was on her mind.

I don't remember what Margie and I talked about that first night, but after a few beers and a round for the house (big spender) I walked back to my apartment with a spring in my step and a smile on my face thinking, "*This is gonna be great!*" One thing I failed to notice on that first visit—and would have given me pause if I had—was a single, but large and unmistakable, bullet hole in the right front plexiglass window just above the Tumble Inn sign.

The next night I brought Leigh down to see what she thought of my new "find." Aside from thinking Margie was kind of cute, the only question Leigh had about my plan was, "*Have you lost your mind?*" While I knew Leigh was smarter than I about most things, I believed strongly in my idea and had a clear vision of what the Tumble Inn could become. After a few more solo visits, I mentioned my idea to Margie. I asked about the lease and whether she was interested in being partners. Since my subsequent visits to the Tumble Inn confirmed my first visit to the bar was not an off night, and Margie's current clientele consisted solely of a handful of old-timers, she *was* interested. She also told me the good news that the Tumble Inn had more than seven years left on its lease and, given the horrific condition of the premises, the rent was quite cheap.

Since I barely had two nickels to rub together (most all my salary from the bank was already spoken for in rent for my apartment and slices of pizza), I had to come up with an attractive offer for Margie that did not involve paying her money I didn't have. What I came up with was simple but perfect. The waterfall for the distribution of the money the new Tumble Inn would hopefully make would be as follows:

- First, all Tumble Inn bills would be paid, including rent, utilities, beer, liquor, bartenders, and other expenses.
- Second, Margie would be paid a salary for managing the bar, which was more than she was currently making.
- Third, Margie and I would split the remaining money equally.

This is the deal Margie and I agreed to and it was the basis for our partnership for the next seven years. Though my day job was still working at Bankers Trust, I sprang into action on my new night job. Leigh, my mother, my father, my brother Arthur, and I cleaned up the place the best we could, but it remained a total dump. Our most ambitious improvement was to paint the bathrooms which were located at the back of the bar, had 10-foot ceilings, and were in such gruesome condition they made you want to either laugh or cry. The walls of the bathroom were original wood lathe and plaster, and pockmarked with holes that looked, disconcertingly, to have been made by fists slamming into them. Margie provided us with a can of fluorescent yellow paint that she said had "*fallen off a truck*" (i.e., been stolen) from a road crew. As we started painting, we quickly realized this paint was intended to be used for the median stripe on roads and was *not* meant for indoor use. We almost passed out from the toxic fumes. We soldiered on, though, and the combination of this paint, and the pockmarks, created a startling visual with the bathroom walls now looking like they were made of radioactive Swiss cheese.

After recovering from the bathroom fiasco, with the little money I had left, I bought a big TV for ball games and stereo equipment for our DJ. The other major piece of hardware the Tumble Inn needed was a huge ice machine which, because I was now out of cash, we leased. We needed a large ice machine because the only coolant in the bar was a tiny refrigerator which looked like it was from the 1940s and could chill only three six-packs of beer at a time.

While the new Tumble Inn might have been short on cash, we were long on ambition, and I planned to be selling beers as quickly as the bartenders could ring 'em up. Rather than pouring money I didn't have into the pathetic infrastructure of the Tumble Inn, I bought 10 forty-gallon rubber trash cans and the high tech magic of beer bottles in trash cans, covered in ice, served the needs of the Tumble Inn perfectly for the next seven years. Of course, we also accommodated fine wine connoisseurs with unrefrigerated white wine, sealed in a rubber bladder, served from a plastic spigot out of a cardboard box.

One amenity we did not provide our customers was food. After business took off, Margie bought a steam cooker and started selling hot dogs in the bar, but I quickly put a stop to it. While I didn't care how sick somebody got from drinking in the Tumble Inn (that was their responsibility and virtually no one was driving), I was unwilling to be responsible for poisoning our customers due to the ridiculously unsanitary conditions of the bar.

Frankly, I don't think it would have mattered if we served our beer warm or poisoned our customers with contaminated hot dogs. After I put my handwritten mimeographed flyers under hundreds of apartment doors in the neighborhood, word-of-mouth began to spread. With a few private parties, Murphy's softball team switching allegiance, and the best college style DJ in town, the Tumble Inn took off like a rocket ship and seemingly nothing could stop us! Some of my favorite memories from the Tumble Inn were when the place was rockin' and Margie would go back behind the bar and put on her show. The Margie Show consisted of serving the assembled masses not only beer, but a full-on dose of her scrappy New York personality. Margie would yell, swear, and generally treat her new customers like the wild animals they were at that moment. I could tell that she loved it as much as any wildcat oilman who, for the first time in many years, hit a gusher and was standing next to his well getting soaked in black gold and happiness.

The Zombies

Unfortunately, as all entrepreneurs will tell you, there are always surprises when you start a new business and those surprises are almost never good ones. In the case of the Tumble Inn the surprise was the reemergence, like a grade B movie, of the Tumble Inn's previous clientele.

While nobody "knew nuttin" about the bullet hole in the front window that greeted visitors, after I got to know the old Tumble Inn patrons I quickly realized it could have been fired by—or at—any of them. Being on the northern edge of the Upper East Side, the neighborhood around the Tumble Inn was dicey. To the immediate south gentrification was in full swing. To the immediate north, however, was a large cluster of low-income housing projects where, I'm sure, most residents were upstanding citizens. However, I came to realize some of the ones who weren't so upstanding used to call the Tumble Inn home. These were the Zombies.

The first few months after the new Tumble Inn opened were a dream. Packed to the rafters every Thursday, Friday, and Saturday night, it was the place to be for young professionals…but then the Zombies arrived to reclaim their old habitat. The Zombies were white males, in their 20s and 30s, who lived in or around the projects. Margie knew all the Zombies, but they were used to her screaming and didn't care much about anything she had to say. Like oil and water, the Zombies and the Preppies did not mix—except to fight. Suddenly my fun neighborhood bar became a Wild West saloon with Zombies and Preppies alternating being thrown out the front door onto First Avenue, picking themselves up, and rushing back in for more. After the new Tumble Inn had been open about six months, things were going from bad to worse. Friends, and friends of friends, were having pool cues and bottles broken over their heads and general mayhem was the order of the day. Something had to be done…but what?

The problem was the Zombies appeared to thrive on mayhem and, although they were outnumbered, they continued to ratchet up their level of violence with no end in sight. From the start, I tried to impose law and order at the Tumble Inn by inserting myself into the role of sheriff. Since I was the owner, and had gotten to know some of the Zombies, my efforts helped modestly. After enough beer, however, neither Preppies nor Zombies were swayed by talk or logic. More than once, as I was putting on my suit and tie to go to work at

Bankers Trust, I looked in the mirror and realized I was sporting a black eye from a melee the previous evening at the Tumble Inn.

Cleanup

Finally, in desperation, I hired the cleanup hitter from our softball team to help me keep the peace. Cleanup was massive; at 6′4″ tall he looked like a preppy version of the Incredible Hulk. Not only did Cleanup look strong, I knew he *was* strong since I had seen him regularly hit softballs so far that today he would be tested for steroids. It was my good fortune that Cleanup was unemployed. He jumped at the chance to be a bouncer at the Tumble Inn and make some money while hanging out drinking free beers with his buddies—Zombie problem solved!

The first time Cleanup reported for duty it was a bitter cold night in mid-December during my first holiday season at the Tumble Inn. I had done some sparse but, quite honestly, pathetic decorating of the bar with a few strings of colored lights and a little tinsel. The overall effect looked more like the handiwork of the Grinch than Santa Claus. To my eye, however, it looked just about right for the Tumble Inn: shabby chic without the chic. It was a Thursday, which was always our biggest night, and Preppies and Zombies started to filter in around 10 p.m. I started to feel pretty good about my newest employee; Cleanup was standing just inside the front door and dwarfed everyone who entered. Just as a warm feeling of security, well-being, and holiday cheer started to spread throughout my body, the bar got mobbed and that night's cycle of drinking, talking, shouting, pushing, and fighting was underway.

As had now become my role, I tried to insert myself into disputes before they got totally out of hand. However, tonight was going to be different because I knew Cleanup had my back. All night long as I played sheriff, I looked over my shoulder for my deputy but Cleanup was nowhere to be found! I weathered that night's chaos the best I could and at 3 a.m., with arctic winds whipping around me, staggered back to my apartment—exhausted from nine hours at Bankers Trust and eight hours at the Tumble Inn—knowing I needed to get up in four hours and do it again. Now, however, I had something new to worry about: hoping Cleanup was okay and the Zombies hadn't done something horrible to him.

The next evening, as we were getting ready to open, Cleanup came by. He sheepishly told me that last night, as he stood in front of the window with the bullet hole and looked at the Zombies who all looked like they carried guns, he decided, "*No job, and no amount of free beer, is worth getting killed for.*"

As Cleanup was telling me this I thought, "*Great…if this guy is too scared to be a bouncer at the Tumble Inn who will?*" I seriously considered closing down the bar right then and there before Cleanup's premonition came true, but I had too much time, energy, and pride invested in the place. Also, the bar was too profitable and too much fun to just walk away. On the other hand, I felt a serious obligation to my customers and friends to not have anyone get killed. I thought about hiring off-duty police to have real law and order in the bar, but that would certainly have changed the free-wheeling atmosphere in the Tumble Inn, and I feared the police would decide the bar itself should be shut down due to all sorts of building code violations (not to mention we were jamming well over 200 people into a building with a legal maximum occupancy of 75).

Just as I was running out of ideas, Leigh came to my rescue. While Leigh initially was unenthusiastic about the Tumble Inn, she now realized what a huge success it had become and she didn't want to see the bar—or me—fail. So Leigh told me what to do to get rid of the Zombies: raise the price of our beer.

When Leigh first suggested this idea I bridled at it because it went against the grain of the friendly and inexpensive neighborhood bar I originally envisioned. However, the Tumble Inn had become more of a nightclub than a neighborhood bar, and desperate times require desperate measures, so a week after Cleanup turned in his badge, the price of beer at the Tumble Inn jumped 30%.

Just as Leigh predicted, the Zombies decided Tumble Inn beer was now too expensive and left to fight somewhere else. The Preppies didn't care how much the beer cost as long as it was cold and there were lots of other Preppies to drink with, and Margie and I tolerated selling more beer at much higher prices. If only all business problems could be solved so simply, effectively, and profitably!

After the Zombies moved on, and the Tumble Inn was no longer serving as the local Octagon, business exploded. The Tumble Inn was a nightclub without a cover charge, velvet rope, or any other pretensions. You went there if you wanted to go crazy with friends and hear great tunes blasted by a great DJ. Very few young professionals who were in Manhattan from 1981 to 1988 would escape the clutches of the Tumble Inn. Over the years, when I meet new people, I have been told countless times, *"You're the guy who did the Tumble Inn…that place was wild…I met my wife/husband there!"*

The Dancing Ceiling

While the Tumble Inn was an intensely public place, some of my most vivid memories of the bar were from when I was there alone. While I did my fair share of bartending, most nights my job was to play host, sheriff, and fireman, rushing around to lend a hand whenever and wherever needed.

Along with the high ceiling, the other positive feature of the Tumble Inn's physical plant was a large basement, lit by a single light bulb, which we shared with a few harmless rats. The basement, though a little scary, was critically important for storing extra cases of beer, since every square inch of the ground floor was taken by the bar, DJ, and customers. (Early on, we took out the tables and chairs to create more space and ultimately the pool table was retired for the same reason. The only furniture that survived were a few bar stools.) As part of my role as fireman, when the party upstairs was going berserk, I would go down into the basement to haul up cases of beer to replenish the supply that was being drunk, spilled, and thrown around in great quantities.

Sometimes while I was in the basement alone, with the pandemonium raging above, I would stop and sit down for a moment on a case of beer to marvel at what was happening. While you could still hear the music pounding above, the basement at those moments had a singular calm only private areas in public spaces can achieve. There was, however, one thing in the basement that was not calm at all—the ceiling—which was active to the point of being frightening.

Like everything in the bar, the floor of the Tumble Inn was ancient. Even when new, I doubt it was built to withstand hundreds of seemingly possessed young men and women jumping up and down simultaneously as our DJ cranked out the hits of Michael Jackson, Bruce Springsteen, and my regular request of The Beatles' "Can't Buy Me Love." The impact this had on the floor was astonishing. When the nights were at their most frenzied, the old wooden floor became like a trampoline and, while you could barely notice it upstairs, in the basement the ceiling would bow down and snap back more than a foot to the beat of the music above.

I did have a few nightmares about the floor giving way, with hundreds of young people landing in the basement and me being interviewed by a nightly news reporter about the tragedy which had just occurred on my watch. Thankfully, that nightmare remained only in my imagination and the Tumble Inn bar, nightclub, and trampoline lasted until the end of the lease, when its tired yet honorable bones were swept away in favor of a high-end grocery store with an apartment tower above.

Six Lessons from the Tumble Inn:

1. Always keep your mind open to new ideas. Before hanging out in Murphy's with the softball team, I *never* considered opening a bar. More specifically, I had just moved to New York, was beginning my career in banking, and was not looking for an outside project. However, an idea occurred to me, I investigated it, came up with a plan, and by putting one foot in front of the other my idea became a reality.

2. One of the first questions smart business veterans ask about any new venture is "*What's your edge?*" This question is shorthand for asking, "*What is so compelling about your product or service that customers are going to want to buy it from you and not one of your competitors?*" In the case of the Tumble Inn, my edge (in addition to finding a failing bar, in a good location, with a cheap lease) was knowing exactly what my clients wanted in a bar and having the ability to reach them directly, and cheaply, with guerilla marketing. (Which means reaching your target audience through word-of-mouth, flyers, or any other form of direct or electronic contact.) This is why it is likely most of your successful entrepreneurial ideas will come from industries you are very familiar with and whose products or services are sold to customers who are similar to you.

3. If you have a great idea for a new business, but you don't have the money needed to get the business up and running, don't be discouraged. In the case of the Tumble Inn, not having much money wasn't an issue because the bar was sinking and my idea was a lifeboat. A more typical situation is for an entrepreneur to raise money from family, friends, or outside investors. Regardless of the specific circumstances, lack of money should *never* be a reason to not pursue an entrepreneurial idea. If you have a great idea, and can sell your ability to execute your business plan efficiently and profitably, there is always money available.

4. It is the rare start-up where the entrepreneur responsible
for the new venture does not, at least once, say to himself,
"*What have I gotten myself into?*" or, even more pointedly, "*If
I could do this all over again—I wouldn't.*" While sometimes
an entrepreneur's worst fears are realized, other times the sun
breaks through. Business is highly unpredictable and it is helpful
for entrepreneurs to know going in they will, almost certainly,
have to deal with unexpected serious problems. Thanks to
Leigh, my Zombie problem got solved, but because of the
Zombies, I learned an important business lesson: "Expect the
unexpected."

5. You will never again have as much energy, and quite possibly
creativity, as you have in your 20s and 30s. Don't believe you are
too inexperienced to take on challenging projects. Energy and
creativity can make up for a lack of experience.

6. It pays to have a significant other who is significantly smarter
than you, loves you, and will look out for you. Leigh saved the
Tumble Inn (by convincing me to raise the price of beer), saved
my career in finance (by convincing me that Wall Street, not
nightclubs, was my destiny), and saved my life (by convincing
the ER doctors I was dying and needed immediate attention).
If you find a partner like that, count your blessings and *never*
let go.

ALL COTTON

Two years after turning the Tumble Inn into the dive bar version
of Studio 54, and while still working at Bankers Trust, a new
entrepreneurial idea hit me. It was 1983 and the 1970s disco era
had just ended. One of the casualties it left behind was a love affair
with polyester clothing—and I hated polyester. Most clothing
available was either entirely synthetic, like disco outfits, or blends of

synthetic and cotton. One could find plenty of khaki pants in stores, however, these pants were almost always blends because the 1970s were also a time when everything had to be "wrinkle free." The result was—except for high-end dress shirts, blue jeans, and painter's pants—there was very little all-cotton clothing available.

My objection to fabric blends had nothing to do with fashion; it was strictly a matter of comfort. To this day, my wanton disregard for my attire is an ongoing source of tension in my marriage (happily, one of the few). I simply love how all-cotton garments feel and hate how blends feel.

Unlike my "aha" moment with the Tumble Inn, my idea for All Cotton slowly dawned on me as I went from store to store in Manhattan, searching in vain, for all-cotton clothing. For someone who didn't care about clothing, I actually got pretty annoyed and that annoyance spurred me into action.

Once I had the idea of starting a retail store that would only sell all-cotton clothing, with the name All Cotton, I knew I had a great deal of work to do before I could get this business off the ground. My first task was to learn about selling clothes. So, while working at Bankers Trust weekdays and helping manage the Tumble Inn Wednesday through Saturday nights, I got another day job, on Saturdays, as a salesperson at a J. McLaughlin store near my apartment.

I chose J. McLaughlin because it was a rare store that did sell cotton clothing. At the time, though, most of their cotton clothes were sweaters. As luck would have it, sweaters were the only article of clothing I didn't like in cotton. To me, the positives of cotton, how it felt, were lost when wearing a sweater over a shirt. Most importantly, when I bought a sweater I expected to wear it a few thousand times and, after a handful of uses, I found cotton sweaters would stretch out and be useless. Regardless, the store sold cotton clothing, and it was near my apartment, so I took the job.

The work itself wasn't bad. The aesthetics of the store were quite nice and the other employees were pleasant. I also liked talking to, and selling sweaters to, customers. What I didn't like was waiting for customers to walk in, and I had no interest in the endless folding and unfolding of sweaters that was required when we were not with customers.

Sweater Girl

What did interest me a great deal was the female manager of the store, whom I will call Sweater Girl. She was about my age, a hard worker, a good manager, and extremely attractive. I had no romantic interest in Sweater Girl because, while not yet married, Leigh and I were very much an item. What I *was* interested in was seeing if Sweater Girl would consider helping make All Cotton become a reality.

After working at J. McLaughlin for two months, I asked Leigh to visit the store so Sweater Girl would know I wasn't hitting on her. Then, I asked her to have lunch with me to discuss an idea. I laid out my plans for All Cotton and I fully expected her to be enthusiastic—but she wasn't. I can't remember Sweater Girl's specific reservations, but I think the real reason she wasn't enthusiastic was she couldn't imagine going into business with someone who quite obviously had no interest in, or talent for, folding sweaters.

Mr. Imagination

The next professional I talked to about All Cotton was a gentleman my mother knew whom I will call Mr. Imagination. When I explained my idea for All Cotton to Mr. Imagination, he had none. As befitting his job as a senior buyer for a major department store, he dressed impeccably. He listened patiently to my pitch and then summarily dismissed the idea as foolish since, "*everyone knows you*

can't have a clothing store that doesn't carry wool clothing." I remember
at the time thinking that was the stupidest thing I ever heard; and
the subsequent success of the Gap, J. Crew, Banana Republic, and
Vineyard Vines, selling virtually *only* all-cotton clothing, in the
exact styles and price points I had envisioned, speaks directly to how
not foolish my idea was.

While I was surprised Sweater Girl and Mr. Imagination didn't
embrace my idea, my confidence in All Cotton hadn't been shaken.
I knew this idea was a winner. However, soon after these two discussions, I decided not to pursue All Cotton. This was because my job
at Bankers Trust was starting to kick into gear and I was beginning
to reap the financial benefits I had hoped from my move into sales
and trading. Also, the Tumble Inn was still going great guns and
I decided these two jobs were as much as I could handle. I must
confess, though, as all-cotton clothing has taken over the world,
I periodically have pangs of regret at having given up on this idea.

Three Lessons from All Cotton:

1. Like the Tumble Inn, my experience with All Cotton is useful
   for understanding the thought process one needs to come up
   with entrepreneurial ideas. Most young entrepreneurs make
   the mistake of asking themselves "*What product or service do I
   want to sell?*" More often, the better question is, "*What product
   or service do I want to buy that I can't easily find?*" If you can
   answer the second question with enthusiasm and conviction,
   it is entirely possible you are on your way to discovering an
   actionable entrepreneurial idea.

2. Often experienced people are "in a box," and it is precisely their
   experience that makes them unable to think creatively. Be particularly skeptical of advice from industry experts who are not
   themselves entrepreneurs. As an entrepreneur, remember it is
   you who has to live with your decisions. So, listen to everyone's
   advice and then trust *your* own judgment.

3. Though I do have pangs of regret about All Cotton, that is different from wishing I had left Wall Street to pursue the idea. This is because I appreciate that the terrific idea I had for All Cotton in no way ensured success. All entrepreneurial ideas fall along a continuum, with the extremes being great ideas which virtually ensure success (Tumble Inn), and equally great ideas that require outstanding execution and some good fortune to succeed (All Cotton). Retail clothing is an enormously competitive business with large, aggressive, and entrenched competitors trained to pivot quickly as fashion changes. Even if I had gotten All Cotton successfully launched, competitors would have copied my products, marketing, and anything else All Cotton did right.

In the face of that stiff competition would All Cotton have survived and thrived? That, of course, is an impossible question to answer, but I believe a good idea and "first mover" status in retail clothing would not have been nearly enough to ensure success. *Everyone understands that in our hyper-competitive free market bad ideas will fail. What is much less well understood is most good ideas will also fail.* To succeed you need the magic combination of a good idea, good timing, good employees, good financial backing, and some good luck. I understand how rare it is for all these "goods" line up to create a highly successful company, and that is why I appreciate my good fortune in joining Greenwich Capital.

GOLFONE

Now you have heard about the Tumble Inn (an idea which became a success), and All Cotton (an idea I did not pursue), it's time to tell you about a business I tried and failed: Golfone. In retrospect, Golfone sounds pretty stupid, but back in early 1992 I was in love with the idea.

Golfone was (or so I thought) an incredibly clever word play (for *golfphone*). In 1992, reasonably few people owned a cell phone, but the technology was catching on. My thesis was, if given the opportunity, busy people who didn't own a cell phone would want to stay in touch while playing golf for several hours, and there would be a *huge* market for cell phone rentals out of golf pro shops.

While working at Greenwich Capital, my plan was to become the golf course cell phone king of the world! I found a partner, I contributed the stupendous idea, and he contributed sweat equity. We hired Andy North, a two-time U.S. Open Champion, to be the "face" of Golfone (our posters in the pro shops were beautiful!), we hired a few salespeople, and we actually signed up 25 clubs in Florida to test the idea. While we did some business, it seemed most people enjoyed the peace and quiet of playing golf without a cell phone. After six months, I made my one *brilliant* decision related to Golfone—I shut it down. Thank goodness I did because within a few years everyone had their own cell phone, and most golf clubs outlawed their use anywhere on their property!

Two Lessons from Golfone:

1. Whenever possible, test your entrepreneurial idea before you go "all in." The 25 clubs we opened in Florida were explicitly done as a test market and when the business did not generate the anticipated revenue, I got out. Testing Golfone saved me a good deal of time, effort, and money—three precious commodities any business person, but especially an entrepreneur, can't afford to waste.

2. One of the many problems with Golfone was that all the funding for the business came from me and I was not the person managing the business day-to-day. If you have a partner in a business venture, the best way you can be certain his interests are aligned with yours is if you are both contributing cash to the enterprise. If your partner doesn't have cash to contribute, you must make sure all incentives and compensation given to him are structured in a way that aligns his interests, as closely

as possible, with yours. For professionals who fund private businesses for a living—called private equity investors—this alignment of interests is one of their most basic and important business principles.

THE STAND

The last story concerning my entrepreneurial activities is out of chronological order. In fact, it takes me way back to when I was eight years old and still living in Lake Forest. I'm including this story because there is an important business lesson here, and because it explains why I felt compelled and empowered to pursue these entrepreneurial dreams while simultaneously trying to climb the steep and slippery corporate ladder.

In the history of American entrepreneurship, perhaps the most famous saying is, "Find a need and fill it." My mother did not coin this phrase, but it was one of her favorites and she regularly repeated it to me when I was eight years old as we strategized, and then executed, a business plan for my lemonade stand. Happily, many children get to have the experience of selling lemonade, but because of my mother, The Stand was something special. Mom loved the lemonade business and she brought the full force of her other favorite saying to the enterprise: "*If something is worth doing, it's worth doing right.*"

Before opening for business, Mom and I went to the grocery store to debate which lemonade and brownie mixes provided the best value for the money and which paper cup sizes were most appropriate for our target clientele. Next, we went to the hardware store and bought a poster board for our sign—carefully keeping all receipts from the recurring cost of goods sold (purchases of the mixes and cups) and our one-time capital expenditure (for the poster board which we would carefully store and reuse).

Next, we sat at the kitchen table, with our lemonade and brownie mixes in front of us, and with pencil and paper calculated precisely how many cups of lemonade and brownie squares our mixes would generate. Finally, we discussed what profit margin the market would bear and what was a fair return for my time and effort. (We settled on two cents for a cup of lemonade and four cents for a brownie.)

Location scouting came next, and no movie director deciding where to shoot his most important scene put more effort into this undertaking. We looked for the most high-traffic area of town, that would have ample parking, be safe from speeding traffic, and be near enough to our house that I could close up shop and ride my bike home if anything bad happened during business hours. After this exhaustive process, we found the perfect spot. It was across from the Texaco gas station and on an active side street that connected the most affluent residential area of town to the village square and shopping district.

The final step Mom and I would go through every summer day was to check the forecast and debate if tomorrow's weather would be hot enough and sunny enough to open The Stand. My Mom and I often disagreed on this judgment call. Consistent with her bedrock belief that commerce was all about finding a need and filling it, Mom would argue that to open The Stand on a cool or cloudy day did not make good business sense, and ran the risk of debasing the high quality brand she was convinced The Stand had established. I had a much simpler business philosophy: I couldn't make any money if The Stand wasn't open.

In retrospect, I believe I had a better innate sense of the market for our product than Mom. The lemonade stand business is as much about selling nostalgia as it is about selling lemonade. While I am certain we would have done less business on cool or cloudy days, I doubt our sales volumes would have plummeted. If I had been able to articulate this thought to Mom, and even if she agreed with my logic, I don't think it would have carried the day. Mom took great pride in The Stand being a *real* business, and business, to Mom, wasn't about selling nostalgia and it sure as heck wasn't about having your hand out looking for charity. Business was about strategy, execution, and offering a square deal to your customers. One thing is certain: The Stand was a rousing success and Mom would often cite this fact as proof her hot sunny day rule was correct. Not having any data from less perfect days, I had no ammunition to fight her on this issue.

No one was more excited by The Stand's success than Mom. When she would come by in our car at our previously agreed upon time in the late afternoon, she couldn't wait to hear how The Stand had done that day. She was equally enthralled by stories about the customers who came by, and what they had said about our lemonade and brownies, as she was by the sales volumes. When Mom and I got back home, a meeting of the finance committee would be held at the kitchen table and we would count the day's revenues. Then I would "get square" with Mom for any outstanding receipts and pocket the profit.

The Stand operated for two summers, until we moved, and I enjoyed everything about it: the strategy and logic which went into each and every decision, the conversations with customers, and the sense of accomplishment from making a profit. However, what I loved most about The Stand was it made Mom proud of me.

RISKS AND REWARDS OF ENTREPRENEURSHIP

This story is about friendship and issues critically important to anyone considering a career as an entrepreneur. It concerns my only close friend who built a complete career as an entrepreneur.

The Surfer

The Surfer and I met through a mutual friend during college and we both ended up at Bankers Trust for our first jobs. We quickly realized we shared many interests. During those first years in New York, we spent considerable time together and we forged the kind of friendship which lasts a lifetime.

The Surfer was a smart and capable guy with many career options. He graduated from Middlebury College and, after three successful years at Bankers Trust, was accepted into Stanford's business school. Traditionally, Stanford has the highest starting salary of any business school, and most of his classmates went on to high-powered jobs which offered the likelihood of very substantial monetary rewards with relatively little personal career risk. Although The Surfer's family was from comfortable circumstances, there weren't sufficient family funds to act as a safety net were he to have a serious financial fall. Regardless, shortly after finishing Stanford, he decided to ride the big and potentially dangerous waves of full-time entrepreneurship.

The Surfer was determined that not only would he start a new business, but his business would revolve around something he was passionate about. He explored a wide variety of ideas and gradually became enthralled with the idea of combining his new athletic love, windsurfing, with his entrepreneurial ambitions.

The sport of windsurfing was small but growing rapidly, and The Surfer saw a business opportunity. His idea was to develop real estate around exotic locales, featuring high winds and warm weather, which were ideally suited to the sport. His plan was to re-create for windsurfing destinations what had been done with high-end ski resorts over the previous 20 years.

Since The Surfer paid for Stanford on his own, with student loans and money saved from Bankers Trust, he was broke. But that didn't faze him. With $20,000 provided by his father, and $20,000 loaned by me, The Surfer grabbed his board and started paddling out into the high seas of commerce—fully expecting to catch some big waves of success.

Despite his optimism The Surfer understood, because he had no track record in real estate development, raising the enormous sums of money needed to purchase land and build infrastructure would have to wait. Instead, he started a travel company and organized trips to established resort areas. From that tiny foothold, he started several of his own windsurfing destination facilities, with the most profitable in Aruba. The original grand vision still seemed far away, but after six years of hard work The Surfer had built a profitable company with several million dollars in seemingly stable top-line revenue. Then everything changed.

Through a series of unfortunate events, The Surfer lost his prime location in Aruba—in a business where location is everything. This problem was not resolved quickly and it drastically reduced the profitability of the business. The Surfer eventually found himself in a very difficult situation. He was eight years out of Stanford, recently married with a child on the way, strapped for money, and was trying to revive a business that was on the ropes. The Surfer put on a brave face, but I could tell he was deeply worried.

Over the next few years, by being smart and resourceful, The Surfer was able to stabilize the business and, with help from the new sport of kite boarding, eke out some growth. He then found a capable manager to run the business which allowed him to focus on other ventures. He eventually sold his company to the manufacturer of the windsurfing and kiteboarding equipment used at his locations. The Surfer was proud of what he built and pleased by the positive ending, but the experience was also sobering. He spent his first 10 years as an entrepreneur pouring his blood, sweat, and tears into building a romantic but risky business which almost derailed his career.

Over the years, The Surfer continued to follow his entrepreneurial passions, but with a more disciplined approach, and one venture in particular stands out in contrast to his first. The Surfer and two partners started a business selling Ugg Boots online. One of his partners came up with the idea and was in charge of operations, one was the website wizard, and The Surfer was the CEO and handled the business issues. While The Surfer recognized a certain magic in these odd-looking sheepskin boots, the idea of selling footwear online wasn't anything he was remotely passionate about. However, he saw what he believed to be a reasonable business opportunity and he quickly became an expert at online marketing.

Almost by definition, it is impossible to know what the next fashion craze will be. (If crazes could be predicted, companies would bring these highly profitable products to market earlier.) So, predictably, The Surfer underestimated the tidal wave of enthusiasm on the horizon for these furry creations. However, when the wave did hit, The Surfer and his partners were perfectly positioned to ride it. Soon, they were shipping nearly $10 million in product and netting over $1 million annually.

After his experience with the windsurfing business, The Surfer realized his time was his most valuable commodity and he needed to maximize it. He left the day-to-day management of the Uggs business to his partners and limited his investment of time to key strategic and management issues. This allowed him to give the Uggs business all the expertise that he uniquely could provide while at the same time leveraging his talents to work on other ventures.

The final chapter occurred a few years ago when, as the CEO and largest shareholder, The Surfer deftly engineered the sale of the business at the crest of the Uggs craze. While selling Uggs was not his only entrepreneurial success, it yielded a remarkable return for the time and energy he spent on it.

There is no doubt entrepreneurship is sexy. In our free market economy the romantic heroes are entrepreneurs. Bill Gates, Steve Jobs, The Surfer's personal hero, Dave McCoy (who singlehandedly built the hugely successful Mammoth Mountain ski resort), and my personal hero, Ted Knetzger (who founded Greenwich Capital), all became rock stars because of the companies they started and the success those companies enjoyed. However, as The Surfer is quick to point out, there is an enormous "survivor bias" for how people think about entrepreneurs—you hear a great deal about wildly successful entrepreneurs, and you don't hear much about the much larger number who fail or barely muddle along.

As The Surfer was about to graduate from Stanford, he and I spent hours on the phone discussing my day job at Bankers Trust and night job at the Tumble Inn. We spent even more time discussing what he should do post-graduation. Since we were both still pretty new to the big leagues, I realize now those conversations were something akin to the blind leading the blind. Recently, I asked him what advice he would give to a young would-be entrepreneur. Here are the five things he said:

1. Pursuing a career as an entrepreneur is a gamble. Despite the risks and difficulties in becoming a successful entrepreneur, for young people with a tolerance for risk and uncertainty, I highly recommend it. There is no feeling quite like using your imagination and creativity to come up with an idea, using your sales and leadership skills to create a business around that idea, and having that business thrive in the harsh reality of the free market. However, being an entrepreneur does not need to be your first act. While some entrepreneurs are anxious to strike out on their own very early in their careers (which is what I did), I recommend you first gain experience working for others in a growing, or dynamic, industry. The more experience you have the easier it

will be to attract big money and top talent needed for most truly substantive ventures.

2. A dedicated entrepreneurial career path is not for everyone. Many of my friends with similar opportunities pursued a more conventional path and, in general, they seem to have enjoyed their careers and found them to be rewarding emotionally and financially. Some of them scratched their entrepreneurial itch as a side interest to their primary careers, and some took the plunge later in life when the risk to their financial security was negligible.

3. Be very conscious of your time. Many entrepreneurs get lost in the battle and are slow to acknowledge reality when a venture is unlikely to develop as originally hoped. Twenty-five years goes by in a flash, and you can't afford to spend a large chunk of it on any business that is not worth your time and effort.

4. My experience with the Ugg business, and Ben's experience with the Tumble Inn, were commercial successes and appropriately leveraged the time we chose to spend on them. However, depending on your goals, these stories could also be misleading. Working on a business part-time is almost never a formula for creating a great and sustainable company. If you have an idea worthy of that goal, understand you will need to focus *all* your energies to make that wonderful dream a reality.

5. In choosing your entrepreneurial ventures, it's okay to consider other personal interests and goals beyond making money. Some people may need an interest or cause beyond making money to give them the determination and incentive to succeed. However, your primary focus needs to be on finding a great business opportunity from a risk/reward standpoint. The free market is exceedingly competitive and unprofitable businesses are no fun to be involved with—even if they revolve around your most passionate interest. Always remember, what is most rewarding is building a successful and profitable business for the benefit of your family, employees, clients, vendors, and the charitable organizations you believe in.

FINAL THOUGHTS

First, be honest with yourself. Are you cut out for the roller coaster that is a start-up or small business? Do you have the determination, funding, and great idea you need to succeed? Both corporate and entrepreneurial jobs will likely be a lot of fun if you are winning. If you are losing neither will be much fun. So, be honest with yourself and decide which platform you think will give you the best chance to win and go with that.

It's Not Just the Company—It's the Job

While you might work at a highly entrepreneurial company, your job might not be entrepreneurial at all—you might be a cog in the machine. Conversely, you could work in a very traditional corporate environment and have an entrepreneurial job where your success or failure (and compensation) is directly tied to your own efforts and achievements. Drawing bright lines about which jobs are entrepreneurial and which jobs are corporate is arbitrary. *My personal definition of an entrepreneurial job/career is any job where you feel a sense of ownership and some combination of your hard work, intelligence, creativity, experience, and leadership can make a significant difference to your company and therefore to your compensation.*

Chapter 3

Being a Leader

If you don't have a job yet, this chapter may seem out of your league. Even if you do have a job, it could be years before you have the chance to formally assume a leadership position—but don't tune out. If you are a college student or young professional without any management responsibilities, you should view this chapter as a window into how your boss thinks. In this chapter you will learn what your boss wants, and doesn't want, from you. This chapter is not organized chronologically. Rather, it contains the information you need to know, especially early in your career, if you want to lead.

WHEN TO BE A LEADER

Numerous times employees have said to me, "*I really want this* (specific) *management position.*" Often, my response is they should first demonstrate leadership at their current job. Invariably, you can identify the leadership potential of people well before they are given a leadership position. Young professionals should realize how few employees consistently show leadership skills. My message to all who have management aspirations is to show your leadership skills well before asking for a leadership position. *In fact, the right time to show leadership is the first day you report to work—and this chapter tells you how.*

LEAD BY EXAMPLE

This is the simplest and most effective form of leadership. *If you work hard every day, and do your job with a great attitude, you are a leader! You need credibility to be a leader and the only certain way to get credibility is to lead by example.*

Player-Coach

My job as the sales manager for U.S. Treasuries at Greenwich Capital was fantastic. If you are ever given the opportunity to be a player-coach, you should be very excited. Being a player-coach allows you to keep producing (for me, this meant continuing to cover a full customer account list) which is great for your credibility with the people who report to you. Also, staying in production makes you a more valuable commodity if you want to switch companies because it is easier to quantify how much your personal efforts contribute to the whole. As you progress upwards in most organizations, there is a centrifugal force to separate you from production. Fight this force as long as you can because once you are cast out into the space of being a non-producer, it is easy to float off into oblivion. Before you leave production for full-time management, make certain you have the *full commitment* of your bosses to make your new management role a success.

BE A LEADER, NOT A MANAGER

Most people are put into leadership positions because they are great at their jobs and are quite intelligent. The problem is, while important, *competency and intelligence don't speak to one important aspect of leadership—whether a person has the ability to inspire others to do their jobs exceptionally well.* Many highly intelligent people feel more comfortable communicating information than they do trying to inspire people. To inspire people, you have to "put yourself out there" and risk being ignored or, worse, ridiculed. Most employees dislike managers but *love* leaders. *Whether they realize it or not, people crave leadership because they want to do their job exceptionally well. Most employees know working hard will be good for their career and much more fun than just slogging through each day.*

One reality for most people in charge of groups, departments, or businesses, is the need for meetings. Most people in charge of meetings spend far too much time sharing information with attendees and not enough time inspiring them. Like any good coach giving a half-time pep talk, you need to understand your strongest "sell" is the last thing you say. For example, if you are a sales manager concluding a meeting about a new product launch, you might say:

> *"Our clients should appreciate this new product is the best in its category and we are committed to its success. Any questions?"*

With the questions out of the way and in a voice 25 percent louder, you lean forward, look everyone in the eyes, and say:

> *"This new product is a big deal for us and will be a big deal for your clients if you sell it aggressively. Let's go get 'em!"*

Or, if you aren't the sales manager, but you are the technology manager, and this is a meeting with your tech guys for the same new product, you could say:

> *"This new product is a big deal for our company. The sales force has been begging us to develop this application and I know we can do it. Let's go get 'em!"*

Remember, the difference between a manager and a leader is a manager tells people what to do and a leader inspires them to want to do it. You owe it to yourself, your co-workers, and the company you work for to be willing to put yourself out there and be a leader.

Don't Talk Until They're Listening

If you want to be a leader, public speaking is important. One trick I learned from watching Ted speak in front of large groups was that he never began until everyone was where he wanted them to be. Most people, if they have to address a large crowd, are nervous and want to be done with the scary undertaking as soon as possible—so they start as quickly as possible. Ted, on the other hand, would always calmly ask those standing to come in closer to him. (If the crowd was seated and there were empty seats up front, he would ask people to move into them.) During this people moving process, Ted would casually banter with individuals, with the result being everyone was put at ease. Once this was accomplished, Ted would ask for everyone's attention. Of course, he hoped this would all happen reasonably quickly. However, he was always willing to wait, with a serene smile on his face, as long as it took to get people where he wanted them to be and as quiet as he needed them to be. Only then would Ted begin.

DON'T BE CYNICAL

As you get exposed to many co-workers, bosses, clients, vendors, and other professionals in the real world, it is easy to get cynical. The reason is most of these people, most of the time, will act in their self-interests. There is nothing nefarious about self-interest. Our entire economic system is built on the premise people will take actions that are in their self-interest. The problem is, a natural reaction to all this self-interest is for you to adopt a cynical "every man for himself" attitude. However, it is very difficult to inspire people and be a leader if you are cynical. People don't trust, and don't want to follow, someone whose day-to-day actions are ruled by obvious self-interest. *If your goal is to be a leader it is in your self-interest to not act in your self-interest.* This paradox is resolved by understanding this short-term sacrifice will ultimately allow you to achieve your long-term goal of becoming a leader.

Once again, Ted provided a wonderful example of how to lead. While consistently acting in the best interests of others, Ted expected, and accepted, that most everyone else would act in their self-interest. He always framed his instructions to individuals or groups to explain why it was in *their* best interest to perform or behave in a certain way. With this approach, Ted was rarely disappointed by people's actions and it allowed him to maintain a positive, noncynical, outlook while living in the real world populated with self-interested human beings. *More than any other character trait, it was Ted's relentless optimism and positive attitude that drew people to him and made him such a natural and effective leader.*

The Best Antidote

Aside from being realistic and generous about what he expected from others, Ted had a powerful antidote to use in battling cynicism. He always believed he had the ability to effect change. After working at Kidder Peabody (a large Wall Street firm) for 10 years, Ted felt his contributions were not being fairly recognized. The reaction of most people would be to get mad and cynical—but not Ted. His response was to leave and start his own firm where he made recognizing each individual's contributions a top priority. *Having the confidence to change what you don't like in your life or career is the single best antidote to the disease of cynicism.* Competing in the big leagues is not easy for anyone—even Ted. Yet he fought all the battles he had to fight while remaining positive and keeping his level of cynicism firmly stuck on zero.

A ROOM FULL OF FOG

Gary Holloway once told me whenever he encountered a new issue or situation, it felt as if he entered a room full of fog. Gradually, as he acquired more information, he would understand the issue better and the fog would lift. As a manager (and even before you become a manager), the best way to dissipate the fog quickly is to use your whole team and ask the right questions of the right people. When a manager calls a group together to work on a project, generally the employees know more about the issue than the manager and that is why they are in the room.

I have often seen senior and junior managers not take the time to listen to the input of the people in the room because they think they know the answer. You can *never* be sure you have the *best* answer until you hear other viewpoints. Being in a management position is a great privilege because you have the ability to snap your fingers and get the expertise you need to make the best possible decisions. Use your experts and remember a good idea is a good idea regardless of whether it comes from a junior, or senior, employee in the company.

Making full use of your team's talents is an underappreciated skill. Knowing what questions to ask, knowing who to ask, and having the intelligence to decide when you are getting good or bad advice is a critical skill for all leaders. This skill is an innate talent some people possess, but it can also be learned. As a leader, don't be afraid to ask simple or "stupid" questions and, if the subject is important, don't ever allow the discussion to move on until you are satisfied you have gotten all the information or advice you need.

Similar to the management of your health care, for important business decisions, always try to get a second, third, or fourth opinion. If you are the boss, employees *love* having you ask for their advice and you may well discover important new information, or an important new perspective on information you already know.

Who Wants to Be a Millionaire

One way to think about this game is the popular TV show *Who Wants to be a Millionaire*. In this show, a contestant wins the $1 million prize if he can answer 14 questions correctly. Each contestant has a small number of "lifelines" to help him answer the questions. The most powerful lifeline is "Ask the Audience" which has an outstanding track record for accuracy. The reason is that the studio audience is large and the collective intelligence of a large group can be astonishing. If contestants were given an infinite number of "Ask the Audience" lifelines, many players would win the top $1 million prize. However, because the number of lifelines are limited, there have been only 11 top prize winners out of over 2,000 episodes. When you become a leader or manager there is no limit to your ability to consult your employees. Use this lifeline often and you will greatly increase your chance to win the game!

Prospecting for Good Advice

Depending on how many people you can go to for advice, and how complex an issue is, the *Millionaire* game show analogy may not be applicable. For some issues a better analogy is panning for gold. In this form of prospecting, one stands at the edge of a river and fills his pan with gravel. Then, with a combination of water, gravity, and skill, the prospector separates the valuable gold from the worthless gravel. As you venture into new personal and professional experiences, you will need to ask many questions and look for the gold in the answers you get back.

Even when you receive advice you believe to be of no value, have enough humility to know you can't always judge correctly which advice is good and which is bad. Also, realize it is a common occurrence for all of us to receive advice we believe is worthless, but during the process of considering this advice we discover, in a form of alchemy, a great solution to our problem.

Finally, be grateful for, and respectful of, the advice you receive. Appreciate when someone is willing to give you advice, and realize it is *your* job to decide if it is good or bad. Be particularly appreciative of negative criticism from people you know care about you. Realize it is much easier to say, "*it's great*" than "*it's not great.*" It is an act of friendship and loyalty for someone to give you negative feedback. Most important, understand your ability to realize your hopes and dreams will be significantly impacted by the energy, focus, and skill you apply to separating the gold from the gravel.

EVERYONE IS IMPORTANT

In order to attain and maintain a position of leadership, it is important to understand *all* employees are valuable to the company and your career. Many people believe if their boss is happy with them everything will be perfect. The reality is your boss's perception of you is largely going to be a reflection of how everybody else in the organization feels about you. If many, or even just a few, people in the company feel negatively towards you then your prospects for advancement diminish. You need to make it clear to each of your co-workers that you are a reasonable person who respects them and the job they do. This attitude should extend from the security guards right up to the CEO. You should care about each of these people—even if only for the selfish reason that they could be important to your career. This dynamic is crucially important and it trips up junior, as well as senior, employees as often as any other issue.

My Friend Kelly

I saw an example of this form of leadership in action early in my career at Bankers Trust from a junior trader, Kelly Doherty. Kelly was my classmate and good friend at Hotchkiss, and he had joined the Foreign Exchange group a year before I arrived on the trading floor. It was obvious Kelly had gotten off to a fast start and he was a highly regarded trader. One evening, as people were starting to leave the floor to go home, I stopped by Kelly's desk to see if he wanted to go out for a beer.

As I waited, Kelly quickly straightened up his desk, but instead of walking out with me he first went around the department and shook hands, or gave a pat on the back, or a goodbye wave with a quick word of appreciation, to each of the 10 or so FX employees remaining at their desks. Most of these employees were clerical staff. This was not the beginning of a two-week vacation for Kelly, nor was it some special day for the department. This was simply Kelly, on his own initiative, thanking his co-workers for their help that day. This was an "*Aha*" moment for me.

The quiet leadership Kelly displayed, even before he became a manager, impressed me immensely. I was not surprised when, at the tender age of 32, Kelly became the youngest member of the Management Committee, nor when, at the age of 37, he became the youngest board member and a vice chairman of Bankers Trust. Compared to Kelly, I was a slow learner, so my personal example of quiet leadership came years later as I was stepping down from 20 years of active duty at Greenwich Capital.

As I was preparing to leave the Co-CEO job at the end of 2006, taking a page out of Ted's playbook, I decided it would be appropriate to write a few letters to the individuals who had been so instrumental to my fantastic experience at Greenwich Capital. The list was short—Ted, Jay, Gary, Chip, Ray Humiston, Morris Sachs, and a handful of others.

After I finished those letters, I realized there were at least 20 more I wanted to write. When I was done with those, the lightbulb switched on: why not write to *every* person whom I had any significant and positive exposure to during my career at Greenwich Capital? I traded in my pen for a recording machine and I started remembering and talking. By the time I was finished three weeks later, I had composed more than 200 letters.

It was an incredible experience, sitting down alone and thinking about each person individually and the funniest, most meaningful, emotional, or successful moments I had with them over the years. Most rewarding, however, are the many times since then when one of those 200 friends has told me how grateful he was to have gotten the letter, how he had shown it to his spouse, and still had it tucked away somewhere.

I always enjoyed the expression "No good deed goes unpunished" because it is often a set up for a funny story. In the real world, however, good deeds are always rewarded by making you feel good, and sometimes they are also rewarded with tangible benefits. In this case, my only motivation to write these thank you letters was just that: to say thanks and have fun retelling old stories. However, three years later when I got back in the game, the time it took to write those letters paid huge dividends when I was recruiting many of my old colleagues from Greenwich Capital to come join me at CRT.

The last four letters I composed during that incredible three-week period were to my wife, Leigh, and my girls, Avery, Kendall, and Cameron. After I unburdened myself and told my work colleagues how much fun I had working with them, and how much I liked and even loved them, I *needed* to do the same for my family.

KNOWING WHAT TO SAY WHEN

"Knowing What to Say When" is the first of five sections in this chapter which revolve around characters I worked with at Greenwich Capital. There are important leadership lessons you can learn from each one and, because I'm sure he wouldn't have it any other way, let me first introduce you to Greenwich Capital's #1 Treasury bond salesman—The Cheese.

The Cheese

He started working at Greenwich Capital a few years after me and nobody really knew for sure why we all started calling him The Cheese, but he insisted it was because he was the Big Cheese! The Cheese was a fascinating study in contradictions. Physically, he was rangy and classically handsome, and on a good day he looked like a young Cary Grant. However, his voice argued against that flattering comparison because he spoke in a high pitch with the quick clipped cadence of a slight exasperated first grade teacher. When he really got going, his pattern of speech resembled the keys of an old fashioned typewriter banging away at a defenseless sheet of paper.

The Cheese was also one of the most intelligent people on a trading floor full of bright folks. However, he regularly would say some of the most ridiculous things imaginable. Finally, The Cheese was perhaps the most egotistical person I ever met. Unlike most egotistical people, though, he generally had a sense of humor about it. Everyone (traders, salespeople, and clients) delighted in making fun of him, but we all wanted to know what The Cheese was thinking because he was always coming up with good trade ideas.

The Cheese and I were quite friendly with never a sharp word between us. I admired the job he did and I think he felt a little sorry for me, and everyone else, because we weren't The Cheese. When I was given the job as sales manager for Treasuries, I became The Cheese's boss. A few weeks into my new job, as I was still recovering from my emergency surgery, Gary Holloway had a big party at his house and The Cheese sought me out to clarify our relationship. As if he was addressing students on the first day of school, The Cheese said, *"Ben, I want you to know that I am going to come to work when I want, leave when I want, go down to the gym and work out when I want, and there is nothing you can do about it."* Hearing this wasn't exactly a shock because you could never anticipate what kind of outrageous things The Cheese would say. However, this declaration by The Cheese did surprise me because he was always the first one in, the last to leave, and never worked out during the day.

While I had been in the big leagues 12 years, I was a rookie manager and I understood this was a "Welcome to the big leagues" test. My authority was being directly challenged by my star player and I knew I had to take this challenge head-on. My response was to look The Cheese straight in the eyes and say in a *very* firm tone of voice, "*Cheese, whatever you want to do is okay with me.*" After that, The Cheese and I, for the next 15 years, continued our streak of never exchanging a sharp word and he continued to be the first one in, the last one to leave, and never worked out during the day.

The lesson here is: When managing people, discretion is often the better part of valor. Even if I later decided to take a harder line, I could have done that by saying, "*Cheese, I was thinking about our conversation the other day and to be fair to the other salespeople I can't allow you to set your own rules.*" That would have been a much better conversation than later being forced to retreat by saying, "*Cheese, I'm sorry about the other night. I've reconsidered and you can do anything you want.*" Don't draw a line in the sand unless you are ready, willing, and able to back it up. To do otherwise is to risk being viewed, accurately, as weak.

The Bear

My experience with The Cheese was an example of managing with a soft touch. My experience with The Bear was the opposite. The Bear was a big bear of a man who had been in the business for more than 20 years, but had been at Greenwich only a few years before I became Co-CEO. What got The Bear into trouble was his attitude towards his junior female sales partner. This young woman, out of desperation, went to HR and complained that The Bear regularly behaved like the boss from hell. The Bear would frequently say inappropriate things in her presence and she felt bullied. However, she did not want to change jobs because she felt she was learning a lot in her current position.

When told about this by HR, I immediately called The Bear into my office and confronted him. The Bear may have had a few issues, but to his credit he wasn't a liar. The Bear put forth a few half-hearted, "*It wasn't that bad*" protests, but he didn't dispute the fundamental facts.

With that clear, I told The Bear, "*This is your lucky day. I'm not going to fire you, but you are going to change your behavior towards your assistant the minute you walk out of my office or else you should keep walking right to the elevators.*" Then I told The Bear the past was the past and going forward all I cared about was that he *always* treat the young woman with the utmost respect. Nothing good would come out of a post-mortem for this kind of issue, so we weren't going to do one. The Bear, seeing I was dead serious, quickly agreed and that was the last I ever heard about him causing anyone trouble.

One Size Doesn't Fit All

For The Cheese and The Bear, my response was dictated less by the personalities involved than by the specifics of the situations. The Cheese was only threatening bad behavior (of a misdemeanor variety), whereas The Bear had already engaged in a serious transgression (bullying a junior employee). In other cases, my response to the same problem could be quite different. For instance, with a highly confident employee who was underperforming, I might take a hard approach and tell him he wasn't all that great, and he needed to prove he was as good as he thought he was. With a less confident employee, who was similarly underperforming, I might tell him how terrific he was and he had nothing he needed to prove to me or anyone else. *If you take the time to understand the psyche of the person involved, and the relevant facts of the situation at hand, you will be well on your way to knowing what to say when.*

DEMAND RESPECT

Most of the time you will earn respect, but at times you must demand it. If you want to be a leader and somebody is being disrespectful to you, do *not* put up with it. If you are out there earning the respect of your co-workers every day this won't happen very often, but in all likelihood it will happen at some point and you should be ready to respond. The first time I felt compelled to address this issue was before I became a manager.

The Brit

On a trading floor filled with larger than average people, The Brit was physically small. However, he had been a star soccer player at Cambridge University and he moved with the confidence and grace of an accomplished athlete. If you met The Brit outside of work he was soft spoken and exuded a bookish, gentle personality. When he sat down at the trading desk, however, he was transformed into a different animal.

The Brit was so determined to make money on every trade he had no governor on his response to losing money. As a trader, just like a pitcher in baseball, you can't "win 'em all" no matter how good you are. However, The Brit wanted to throw a no-hitter every day and when he did give up some hits he would often freak out, heaping abuse on the salesperson, or occasionally a trader, whom he felt were responsible for his loss. Sometimes The Brit had reasonable grounds for his diatribes and sometimes he didn't. Regardless, The Brit was unique in the ferocity of abuse he periodically directed at the sales force.

The Brit and I always had a good professional relationship until one day and one trade. My memory of the offending trade is long gone, but what happened next I remember clearly. The Brit, having lost money on one of my client's trades, unleashed his wrath on me. I was startled, embarrassed, and hurt. The Brit had never treated me this way before and as I wrote up the trade ticket, I thought about how to respond.

As I laid the ticket on The Brit's desk, I leaned over and whispered in his ear, "*If you ever do that to me again in public our relationship is going to change drastically.*" Now it was The Brit's turn to be startled, not because I stood up for myself, but because the trade happened three minutes before and by the time I whispered in his ear he had already forgotten about it! Nevertheless, The Brit got the message loud and clear and that incident was the only time he ever directed his verbal assaults at me.

The lesson here is: If you have ambitions to be a leader, it is important you treat everyone with respect at all times and you insist on being treated with respect. It is difficult to lead if your co-workers see you don't insist on being respected.

There is an interesting postscript to this story. A couple of years later, during my ill-fated tenure as a trader, I was desperately looking for guidance and coaching from the experienced and successful traders on the floor. The most help I received was from my good friend and deskmate, Morris Sachs, but The Brit also was enormously generous to me with his time and advice. As with many extremely talented people, The Brit had a complex personality and I will always remember him as much for his help and support, when I needed it most, as for his extraordinary tirades.

MAKE THE WHOLE GREATER

In many ways, making the whole greater is the essence of building and growing a company. The following is one example of how employees and managers can achieve this goal.

Blue

Blue was my first hire when I became a sales manager at Greenwich Capital. He was an old college friend who got his nickname—mainly used by his three older brothers and picked up by me—because as a kid he loved blue popsicles. Blue spun his wheels for a few years after college, but eventually he became a very successful Treasury bond salesman at J.P. Morgan. When I tried to lure Blue to Greenwich Capital, it was more difficult than I anticipated because he liked J.P. Morgan and was doing extremely well there.

When I left Morgan Stanley I had no children—it was just Leigh and me. By 1992, however, Blue had a wife and two small children to worry about, and the idea of leaving the safety and security of J.P. Morgan for a small firm was frightening. The day he finally gathered his courage to resign from J.P. Morgan, he had no idea what was in store for him. Although I had been at Morgan Stanley for less than a year, I was forced to go a few rounds with John Mack before I could get out the door. Blue, on the other hand, had been at J.P. Morgan eight years, was one of their top producers, and considered to be a true blue Morgan Guy.

When Blue tried to resign he was given the full-blown Wall Street treatment. First, they put him in lockdown in a conference room. Next, wave after wave of J.P. Morgan managers tag teamed, playing good cop/bad cop, to work him over. They told Blue what a disastrous decision he was making, how much they all loved him, and how he was betraying the entire J.P. Morgan team.

However, even a huge organization like J.P. Morgan's fixed income department has only so many managers. After four hours, they'd all taken their best shots and Blue was finally allowed to leave the building.

Immediately, he went to the nearest pay phone and called me for reassurance that he was doing the right thing. He sounded shaken. Scores of people he had worked with for eight years telling him what a huge mistake he was making had taken its toll. Over the phone, I could feel Blue's resolve melting, and I feared he might turn around and walk right back into the job he just left. I knew Blue's concerns all revolved around being able to financially take care of his family, and I desperately racked my brain for something to say to address the issue. At that critical moment, the best I could come up with was "*Blue, don't kid yourself. None of those guys were looking after your best interests. Get your ass up to Greenwich right now and by the time you go home for dinner tonight you'll be blowing your nose with hundred dollar bills.*" Though crass, that did the trick and an hour later Blue was sitting at his new desk. While I don't know how much money Blue made selling bonds at Greenwich Capital that first afternoon, I do know, in short order, he was making double what J.P. Morgan ever paid him and that happy situation lasted for the next 17 years.

At Greenwich, Blue was rock solid. He arrived early, stayed late, and performed well every day. He always had a positive attitude, a smile on his face, and a funny story to tell when business got slow. While not quite as large a producer as The Cheese, Blue made every bit as large a contribution to the firm's success because he was a critical part of the glue that held our group together and made it fun to come to work each day.

Many superstars have such strong personalities they seem to create their own highly volatile microclimate. If these superstars are happy, you can feel the sun shining and the birds chirping sweetly around them. However, if these superstars are unhappy, you can almost see the clouds roll in, hear the thunder booming around them, and feel the lightning bolts threaten all who dare to come near. Fortunately for Greenwich Capital, the microclimate around Blue was always warm with clear blue skies.

Three Lessons from Blue:

1. It is the oldest trick in the book for managers of a valued long-term employee to attempt to guilt that employee into staying. Management can make many legitimate arguments to an employee to get him to reconsider leaving, but guilt is not one of them. *All you owe your company is your best effort while you work there.* Beyond that, your only obligations are to your dependents (if you have any) and to your personal hopes and dreams.

2. All my moves, up to and including joining Greenwich Capital, occurred before Leigh and I started a family. For most people, it generally takes at least a few tries to find the best company to pursue their career. The easiest time to aggressively seek out the best company to match your personality and talents is when you are young and before you have children. While Blue finally did take the risk to join Greenwich Capital, the decision was much tougher than if he moved earlier.

3. Every successful organization needs a backbone of strong professionals who become stars by helping make the whole greater than the sum of its parts.

THE GUIDING PRINCIPLE

Business issues can be so complex, and at times confusing, it is important to have a guiding principle you can always turn to in the decision-making process. During my career, some of the most emotional and pressure-packed decisions I had to make concerned which salesperson should cover which account. As with most disputes on Wall Street, on the surface it appeared that people were arguing over money (in this case, potential sales commissions).

However, at least as important as the money was the perceived respect (or lack thereof) involved.

One Way

One Way was the Mortgage Department's version of The Cheese—their #1 salesman. Like The Cheese, he was tall and good looking. While The Cheese relied on his intelligence and relentless nagging to get the job done, One Way's weapon was his force of personality. When One Way wanted to be, he was almost as charming as Ted, and in some ways, as a pure salesman, he was better. Like all great salesmen, it was not so much what One Way said, but how he said it. When he spoke, you immediately felt you were talking to the most rational and honest person you ever met. After the first time I sat down and talked to One Way, I would happily have made him executor of my will and guardian of my children. He had a truly remarkable ability to inspire trust and goodwill.

In addition to being the #1 Mortgage Department salesperson, One Way was also one of Greenwich Capital's regional sales managers, and he joined our firm a few years before Jay and I became Co-CEO's. At Greenwich, because of Ted's performance-based compensation plan, we generally didn't spend a lot of time arguing about compensation. However, there *were* occasional knock-down, drag-out fights over who would cover which accounts. Most of the time these disputes were handled by the sales managers, but when conflicts couldn't be resolved peacefully, I always encouraged the parties involved to come to me before conflicts got out of hand. As a regional sales manager, it was One Way's job to represent his salespeople in account disputes and, as you might guess from the name I gave him, One Way saw things…well, one way.

The first issue I mediated that involved One Way was an account dispute with a very senior, very productive, and very well-liked

Treasury salesman. This salesman had been covering his best account for many years and had strong and deep relationships throughout that large organization. Recently, in addition to Treasury bonds, the account had started to buy and sell mortgage bonds with the Treasury salesman. When One Way got wind of this, he requested the account be covered for mortgages by one of the mortgage salesmen in his office. This was an entirely reasonable request since both Greenwich Capital, and I, believed in "specialist coverage." The time and focus it took to understand either the market dynamics driving Treasury bonds, or the complex structures of mortgage bonds, made it impossible for a "generalist" salesperson to provide the best cover to his clients—and we were determined to provide all our clients with the best coverage on Wall Street.

Normally, this decision would have been easy and One Way would have prevailed. However, in this case, the company's portfolio manager who traded mortgages had specifically and forcefully requested that the Treasury salesman cover the account for both Treasury and mortgage bonds. Again, the decision appeared to be easy—but this time with the Treasury salesman prevailing because the one guiding principle I applied to all issues was: do whatever is in the best long-term interest of Greenwich Capital. (By the way, I don't take any great credit for understanding that it was virtually always in our firm's best interest *not* to defy a client's clearly expressed wishes on who should cover their account.)

Despite these undisputed facts, One Way requested a meeting with the Treasury salesman and me. Since this was my first encounter of this sort with One Way, I had no doubt that this smart, charming, and great guy would quickly understand the logic of allowing the Treasury salesman to continue covering the account for mortgages. However, I hadn't been involved in all the back and forth with the client, so I remained open to the possibility there was additional information that could change my mind.

One Way, the Treasury salesman, and I met in a glass-faced conference room on the edge of the trade floor. It quickly became clear that One Way had no new information concerning the issue at hand. However, he did have some definitive thoughts on the account assignment issue. He launched into his view of the situation saying, "*Greenwich Capital has policy of specialist coverage for all products and the fact that this client has requested the Treasury salesman cover him for mortgages should not matter. The Treasury salesman is not knowledgeable enough about mortgages and my salesman should be put on the account. It is the Treasury salesman's job to get the account to agree to this. If he can't get this done then maybe his relationship with the client isn't all that good, and that would be one more reason to assign my salesman to the account.*"

Whoa! You could have knocked me over with a feather. What happened to that charming great guy I had recently talked to? While it took me a moment to get my bearings back, the Treasury salesman was quicker on the uptake and, having been on Wall Street for many years, he knew an insult when he heard it. He immediately began swearing loudly at One Way, using every curse word in the book. It got so bad, so quickly, that a good portion of the trading floor was staring into the conference room wondering what the hell was going on. After almost a minute of this tirade (which felt like an hour), I realized the Treasury salesman wasn't going to stop shouting expletives. I then grabbed him, told him the meeting was over, and that he better get a grip—all the while privately being in sympathy with him about the wildly inflammatory manner One Way had chosen to express his position. Later, when the Treasury salesman did get it together, I ruled in his favor and he continued to cover the account for mortgages. The only stipulation I made was that the Treasury salesman had to continue to try to convince the client that it was in the client's best interest to have a mortgage specialist cover their account for that product.

A year later, using his substantial influence with the account, the Treasury salesman *was* able to convince the client to accept a specialist salesperson for mortgages. This was exactly how the process was meant to work: respect the client's wishes, respect our salesmen's established relationships with clients, and encourage salesmen to work for the best long-term interests of the firm. While a mortgage specialist eventually did get assigned to the account, that salesman was not from One Way's office. This decision was made, at least in part, because One Way's previous intransigence on this issue had poisoned the well with both the Treasury salesman and the account. For such a smart guy, it was crazy One Way had chosen a path that had *no way* for him to get his desired outcome.

The epilogue to this story is that One Way remained at Greenwich Capital for more than 10 years, and he continued to be an outstanding salesman and respected leader within his regional office. His Achilles heel, however, continued to be his inability, or unwillingness, to see issues from any perspective other than that which most benefitted him or his direct reports. This flaw dogged One Way throughout his career at Greenwich Capital and diminished the credibility he had, and the influence he wielded, outside of his regional office.

The lesson here is: When you become a manager, you do become an advocate for your team; however, that does not mean you put the interest of your team above those of the firm. Many managers approach their job as if they were defense attorneys—making whatever arguments and taking whatever actions—to further the interests of their departments. This approach to managing is both very common and very wrong. In fact, this is one of the most misguided and damaging mistakes otherwise talented managers regularly make. *The guiding principle for all managers must be "firm first."* Only after that box is checked should a manager engage in their secondary (but nevertheless very important) job of being an advocate for their team.

LEADERSHIP, FRIENDSHIP, AND ADVERSITY

The last character I am going to introduce you to in this chapter is my good friend Marble. If misguided priorities held One Way back from fully realizing his leadership potential at Greenwich Capital, Marble encountered a very different problem with the same unfortunate result for the firm.

Marble

I don't know who at Greenwich Capital came up with his nickname, but some nicknames are so perfect they stick immediately—and Marble was one of those. It was perfect because he was like a block of stone. Everything about Marble was square: his head, his neck, his shoulders, right down to his toes. He was six feet three inches tall, blond and fair-skinned, without an ounce of fat. If he had chosen to be an actor rather than a bond salesman, he would have been typecast as a drill sergeant.

I knew Marble before Greenwich Capital; I was two classes ahead of him at Bowdoin. Even in college, he stood out by seeming to be much more "squared away" than the rest of us. Given our age gap, and the fact that we were in different fraternities and played different sports, I didn't know him well back then. My most vivid memories were watching Marble play varsity basketball and seeing him rip down rebounds like a man possessed. He was not someone you wanted to mess with.

Many people helped me along the way and were generous with their time and unstinting in their support. The people who were my most important mentors were Ted Knetzger and Gary Holloway. The person I helped the most was Marble. Our close relationship started after Marble graduated from Bowdoin and got a job at Bankers Trust in the same commercial lending program I had been in two years earlier. I contacted him and encouraged him to join my department, the Middle Market Lending Group, because I believed you could learn more about business and banking by lending money to smaller, less established companies than to bigger companies. After hearing my pitch, Marble did join the Middle Market Group, but he was assigned to a different office.

Soon after I got my transfer to the sales and trading department of Bankers Trust, I called Marble and told him he belonged downtown. I knew he would be an awesome salesman and a few months later Marble was on the trading floor with me in Treasury bond sales. After I joined Greenwich Capital, I again called Marble and explained he could make more money and have more fun at Greenwich Capital and, again, he listened to me and we were reunited, sitting next to each other.

By the time Marble arrived at Greenwich, he was already a great salesman: determined, intelligent, and fearless. He fit right in with the all-star team Ted had assembled and, like me a few years earlier, Marble quickly knew he had found his professional home. From the moment he arrived it was clear he would become "a player" at the firm. As I was moving from sales to trading in 1990, Marble was the logical person to take over some of my biggest accounts. This handoff fit both of us perfectly. Marble got a few new large clients and I knew these clients would be well taken care of.

Two years later, as I was getting out of the hospital and returning as the sales manager, Marble showed the quality of person he was. Since my job was to be a producing sales manager, I needed some accounts to cover. However, my old accounts were already being covered, with the largest ones covered by Marble. Entirely on his own, with no request or pressure from anyone, he volunteered to swap seats with me and become a trader. I slid right back into my old seat, with my old clients, plus the addition of Marble's accounts.

Marble planned to leave sales at some point to trade or manage, but he had intended to make that move a number of years down the road, as he was making great money, covering great accounts, and life was good. However, Marble dramatically fast-forwarded his plans in order to make my transition back into sales easier. This was quite a role reversal with my mentee suddenly taking care of me. In my experience as a producer and manager, having Marble give up his valuable sales seat to me was an unprecedented act of friendship, loyalty, and selflessness.

Marble's positive personal and professional traits translated into leadership qualities. After trading for a short time, he was asked to go to London to build out and run our European business. Greenwich Capital was late in opening a London office and our operations there were barely treading water with a tiny office and lousy technology. That was all about to change.

When Marble arrived in London sparks began to fly. He was a man on a mission: he identified a great young technology guy in our Greenwich office and convinced him to move to London, he convinced our trading heads to send over some of their best guys, and he opened a beautiful new office in Piccadilly Square. Marble was out every night either recruiting local sales and trading talent to join the London office, or entertaining our now booming European client business with his salespeople and traders. Marble was unstoppable and, while he could occasionally be a bull in a china shop, everyone at the home office was delighted with what he was accomplishing. Then NatWest bought Greenwich Capital.

On the surface, being bought by NatWest (a large London bank) looked like a good thing for Marble—but it wasn't. As is common in acquisitions, there were many conflicts between the two organizations and the epicenter of these conflicts was Marble's London office. As tensions between the two firms escalated, Marble, because of his position and strong personality, was asked to defend

Greenwich Capital's interests. Daily, Marble would grab the
Greenwich Capital flag, wave it over his head, and charge up the hill
with no regard for the heavy artillery positioned directly in front
of him.

The problem was that although our businesses were world-class,
and the overlapping businesses at NatWest were also-rans, it was
not a fair fight. While Greenwich Capital operated autonomously,
NatWest was our parent company and the senior management of
NatWest (who controlled the heavy artillery) would, at the end of
the day, support their guys in London over the Greenwich guys.
Things reached a crescendo in 1998, and it seemed an all-out war
could break out at any minute.

My take on the situation was that the management of Greenwich Capital, knowing full well who would lose the war, attempted
to defuse the situation. Marble, who had come to symbolize
everything the Brits hated about the Yanks, would have to go.
When a senior Greenwich manager told me Marble was going to be
fired as the head of the London office, I protested, but it was clear
the decision had been made and it was not open for discussion.
What this manager said to me was, "*Ben, you have only one choice to
make…you can get on a plane and go over to London and tell Marble
he is no longer the head of the London office, or else I'll call him.*" My
first instinct was to say, "*Good luck with the call,*" but I did think
Marble deserved to hear the news from someone in person, so I
agreed to go.

When I arrived at our office in Piccadilly, Marble smelled a rat.
He knew there was no good reason I scheduled a trip to London on
one-day's notice and, while he was glad to see his good friend, I could
tell he was thinking, "*What the hell is Ben doing here?*" We sat down in
his office and, never one to beat around the bush, I said, "*Marble, I've
come over to tell you that you're fired.*" I intended in my next few sentences to tell him I thought this was a bad decision, I thought he had

done a *great* job in London, and I thought the whole thing sucked. However, before I could utter another word, I could see that Marble's head was about to explode and suddenly my only thought was, "*I'm going to die.*" He had that wild look on his face I recognized from the basketball court, but now instead of ripping a rebound off the backboard, I feared he was going to rip my head off my shoulders and throw it down the length of his beautiful new trading floor. While Marble didn't physically assault me, he did hurt me when, seething with anger, he said, "*Okay, now you've proved how tough you are to the guys back in Greenwich—why don't you get the hell out of here.*" I shot back at him, "*Hey, the only reason I came over to London was because of our friendship. I think you're getting a totally raw deal, but if you think I'm here for any other reason except that I care about you—you're out of your mind.*" Immediately, the tension was broken as Marble realized I was on his side in this ugly situation. With that behind us we went out, got drunk, and resumed our close friendship. (To be precise, Marble had not, technically, been fired from Greenwich Capital. He was simply being removed from his position as the head of the London office. However, both Marble and I knew this was a distinction without a difference since his interest at that point in his career was to build a business and there were no such opportunities available back in Greenwich.)

The big loser in all this was not Marble—it was Greenwich Capital. We lost an incredible salesman and leader. After I became Co-CEO in 2000, I tried to rehire Marble, but by then he had become more interested in the buy-side (managing money and thus being a customer of Wall Street), and I was unable to lure him back. Predictably, Marble has gone on to bigger and better by founding and running a very successful private equity firm.

Four Lessons from Marble's Story:

1. The efforts and leadership of a single individual can bring about remarkable results. While the London office remained a modest

part of Greenwich Capital's overall business, Marble brought an energy to that office which was solely due to his focus, talent, and determination. If not for NatWest, I am confident that both Marble's career, and the fortunes of our London office, would have continued their dramatic ascent.

2. In business, friendships are valuable, but close friendships are invaluable. Close friends are like family and will do anything in their power to help you. As I was returning to sales and Marble volunteered to give up his seat for me, he said in his classic 100% certain tone of voice, "*I wouldn't do this for anyone else.*" I knew that was true. I also understand how critical that act of generosity was in paving the way for my successful return to sales—which set the stage for my future promotions.

3. While the NatWest situation wasn't Marble's fault, his strength may have been his weakness. Marble was a force of nature who lacked some of the self-preservation instincts one periodically needs in order to understand when to back off in order to fight another day. Consistent with his personality, perhaps Marble knew full well the sands were shifting under his feet, and he just didn't care. I'm not sure. What I am sure of is, throughout *your* career, you need to keep your head on a swivel to look out for people, issues, or situations, that could run you over.

4. Being fired as the head of the London office was a "Welcome to the big leagues" moment for Marble. The fastball hit him square on and knocked him to the ground. But so what? The important thing is he immediately got back up, dusted himself off, and went on to play the game so well he now owns his own team. To recover as Marble did, and keep moving forward, is an act of courage and a great example of how to survive and thrive in the big leagues.

THE LEAST FUN PART OF THE JOB

While I was in various leadership positions at Greenwich Capital, a number of times friends and employees said to me sympathetically, "*You must hate having everyone come to you with all their problems.*" My response was always, "*No, I actually enjoy it.*" I doubt many people believed me, but it was true. For me, "people problems" were almost always interesting and I enjoyed being called upon to help solve them. However, there was one category of problems I never enjoyed: firing people. I hated firing people and I always needed to give myself a pep talk before doing it. My internal dialog went something like this:

> "You have a solemn responsibility to all the people who work for you to keep Greenwich Capital as healthy and profitable as possible in order to pay all employees for their talents and hard work. Also, the pain you feel in firing someone is only a tiny fraction of the pain that person will feel. So stop whining and do your job. If you can't do this, you need to hand over this job to someone who is willing to make these tough decisions."

After that I would call the person into my office, tell him they were being let go, and try to gently explain why. If I got pushback, I *never* tried to convince the person that I was doing the right thing. This moment was painful enough for him without me arguing my case against him or citing the fact that others agreed with this judgment (which was always the case). Rather, I would invariably respond to their counter-arguments saying, "*You may be right. I make plenty of mistakes and this could well be one of them. However, it is my job to make these decisions and this is what I decided. I'm very sorry.*" This felt right for me to say because:

- It was the God's honest truth. I might be making a mistake.

- It was unnecessary to argue the point because I had the power (and I believed the obligation) to do what I was doing.

- It eliminated the need to kick a person when he was down by going into gory detail why he was being fired and who all agreed with the decision.

- It was a position against which there was no argument. The decision had been made, and the only thing left to do was accept it and move the discussion forward to items such as timing, announcement, and severance.

My dislike for firing people was not the principal reason I eventually became less enthusiastic about managing Greenwich Capital day-to-day, but it certainly was a contributing factor. Though we had much greater stability of personnel and management at Greenwich Capital than the typical Wall Street firm (and thus less firing to do), after my 14 years in leadership roles, I nevertheless had more than enough of it to last a lifetime. The truth is, firing people is a type of "creative destruction" which is central to capitalism and free markets. But that's economic theory. In the real world, it's painful for everyone involved.

One thing you need to understand when people get fired: it often is not a reflection on their abilities. All it means is that particular person was, or was judged to be, not the right person for the job they were in at that time. This was especially true at Greenwich Capital where most everyone was a top professional to begin with. The proof of this was the not insignificant number of employees who were fired by Greenwich Capital and went on to enjoy great success at other firms where they were in the right job at the right time.

TOO MUCH CREDIT—TOO MUCH BLAME

The leadership of a company is rarely as good, or as bad, as they are portrayed. People inside and outside the company invent story lines to conform to outcomes. While Greenwich Capital outperformed its peers in the early to mid 2000s, most all of Wall Street had a good run during that stretch of time. The result was the senior management of the major Wall Street firms were considered to be "Masters of the Universe." However, by 2008, these same individuals were roundly considered to be incompetent buffoons (or worse).

The truth is: these were the same people—doing the same things—they had been doing prior to 2008. So what changed? The market changed. During the boom times top management was pushed by stockholders, employees, and clients—as well as their own egos and perhaps greed—to take more and more risk. While the music played (rising real estate prices), everyone danced and was happy. When the music stopped (falling real estate prices), most of Wall Street, including Greenwich Capital, stopped dancing.

A more honest evaluation of Wall Street senior management during the 2000s is that they were never geniuses and they were never buffoons. Rather, they were simply human beings who put their pants on one leg at a time and whose performance was at least as much determined by factors outside their control (like rising or falling markets) as by factors within their control (the actions they took).

This phenomenon of too much credit and too much blame is in no way limited to Wall Street. It is hugely present in all businesses as well as in all sports. *When you win, you are admired and considered to be virtuous. When you lose, you are denounced and considered to be a bum: "Welcome to the big leagues."* When you become a leader, it is also important you remember this lesson so you don't get too high on yourself when things go well—or too down on yourself when things go poorly.

Chapter 4

Staying Out of Trouble

I n the big leagues, trouble is anything that gets in the way of you accomplishing your goals. While trouble can come in an infinite variety of shapes and sizes, the following are eight stories of how I, and others, have gotten into trouble in our careers and what you can learn from our mistakes. These stories are ordered chronologically and span virtually my entire Wall Street career—starting with me being bitten by a RAT on the trading floor of Bankers Trust.

RAT BITE

It was 1983 and I had just arrived on the trading floor as a junior Treasury salesperson. I had gone through a brief sales and trading training program, but I barely knew my way to the bathroom, much less anything about the highly specialized world of selling and trading U.S. Treasury bonds. Before I would be entrusted with real live clients, my assignment was to learn the business by shadowing veteran salespeople. Late one Friday afternoon, after I had been on the floor only a few weeks, the direct dial line ominously labeled RAT began blinking. By then, even I knew The RAT was the Merrill Lynch Ready Asset Trust money market fund—one of Bankers Trust's biggest, most aggressive, and most important clients. The RAT was covered by one of BT's senior salespeople, Joe McCarthy, whom I happened to be shadowing and who had left early. On his way out the door, Joe told me to answer his phone and take any messages.

As The RAT continued blinking, I looked around desperately hoping someone else would pick up the phone—but no such luck. Everyone was either gone or busy, so, with more than a little trepidation, I picked up the phone and said, "*Hello?*" There was half a second pause on the other end of the line and then The RAT let me have it, "*WHO THE FUCK ARE YOU AND WHERE'S JOE?*" I stammered something about Joe being gone for the day and asked if I could help. The next thing I heard was The RAT screaming, "*I NEED TO MAKE A LATE DELIVERY ON BLAH, BLAH, BLAH.*" I say blah, blah, blah because that is how it sounded to me. I had no idea what The RAT was talking about and no idea what he wanted me to do, so, thinking quickly on my feet, I replied, "*What?*"

That's when I'm sure The RAT started salivating and he went in for the kill by screaming even louder, "*ARE YOU GOING TO HELP ME OR NOT—I NEED TO KNOW RIGHT NOW!*" I replied honestly "*I don't know what you want me to do.*" Then The RAT stopped screaming and, exaggerating the enunciation of each word, replied slowly but with an intensity that jumped through the phone line and grabbed me by the front of my shirt collar, "*Say-you'll-take-my-late-delivery.*" After sitting with salespeople for the past few weeks, it appeared to me the only thing salespeople ever said to their clients was "*Yes,*" and, with no help to be found, I said "*Okay*" and clicked off the line.

I sat there for a moment and tried to figure out what just happened, but quickly gave up and went to find someone who might know. Soon I was in front of the head of the trading desk, Bill Feezer, telling my story about the late delivery I had just agreed to. Now it was Feezer's turn to say "*What?*" Seconds later, Feezer was in Joe's seat talking to The RAT, with me sitting next to him, and a small crowd gathered around rubbernecking the accident to see how bad it was.

When Feezer hung up, he took a calculator out of his pocket, punched a few numbers, looked at me and said calmly, "*Because the delivery was late, we can't settle these bonds with the customer we sold them to until Monday, and it will cost us $25,000 in interest to hold these bonds over the weekend.*" Standing behind me was a trader from the Treasury financing desk where my newly minted $25,000 loss would be recorded, and he exploded, "*That's ridiculous; the kid had no idea what he was agreeing to—we should cancel the trade.*" Almost before the trader could finish his sentence, Feezer, raising his voice for the first time, sharply cut him off: "*When he picked up this phone he was speaking for all of us.*" Then Feezer stood up slowly, put his hand on my slumping shoulder, and said quietly, "*Don't worry about it—just learn from it,*" and walked away.

Being bitten by The RAT taught me three important "Welcome to the big leagues" lessons:

1. Don't ever agree to anything you don't fully understand. This lesson is as important in your personal dealings as it is in your professional career. My Greenwich Capital partner, Jay Levine, is fond of saying, "*If you don't know who the sucker in the room is—it's you.*" Not fully understanding what you are agreeing to is the definition of being a sucker and, believe me, you *don't* want to be that person.

2. The sum of $25,000 was almost exactly my annual salary. When Feezer told me my mistake cost Bankers Trust that amount, I saw my fledgling career on Wall Street flash before my eyes. I have been eternally grateful to Bill Feezer for the support he showed me that day, and I have attempted to show the same support to junior employees when they make mistakes which, while perhaps stupid, are honest ones they can learn from.

3. Feezer's generosity in quickly moving on allowed me to do the same. As with errors in sports, what's done is done, and the only thing to do is get back out there and focus on helping your team score the next goal.

GET SOME GODDAMN SLEEP!

A year after being bitten by the RAT, I was still actively managing the Tumble Inn as well as doing my job as a bond salesman at Bankers Trust. Either of these jobs amounted to a full-time commitment, and together they were the ultimate "burning the candle at both ends." I did not fully appreciate this problem until my sales manager, Pat Alexander, came by my desk one day and sat down next to me.

Pat: *How you doin' Ben?*

Me: *Okay I guess.*

Pat: *You don't seem okay to me.*

Me: *What?*

Pat: *Ben, you're dead on your feet and I'm not the only one to notice it…what's going on?*

Me: *Well, you know, I got this bar and…*

Pat (cutting me off): *Is the bar more important to you than this job?*

Me: *Well no, but…*

Pat (again cutting me off and now practically yelling at me): *Well then get some goddamn sleep!*

After Pat walked away, I was stunned. He was a great guy whom I liked and respected, and he was normally quite mild-mannered. While I stayed involved with the Tumble Inn for another six years, I significantly cut back my hours at the bar. I realized Pat just called "strike one" on me, and if there was a second strike I would likely be thrown off the team.

If you are working full-time, you need to appreciate that any significant outside responsibilities or projects you take on run the risk of diminishing the quality of the work you do at your full-time job. These other responsibilities or projects could include:

- Starting an entrepreneurial venture like the Tumble Inn.
- Going to business school at night.
- Starting a family.
- Being the primary care person for a loved one.
- Other responsibilities or projects (like writing a book) which take a significant amount of your time, energy, or focus.

Given how I conducted my career, I would be the wrong person to tell you not to take on additional responsibilities or projects; however, you do need to understand your full-time boss expects to have your full-time effort and attention. The truth is there are more fun, interesting, and worthwhile things out there than you will have time for. You will have to make choices. Thinking it through carefully and making the right choices, is critical to surviving, thriving, and having fun in the big leagues.

FRONT PAGE NEWS

When I began at Greenwich Capital, Gary Holloway used to tell us, *"Don't ever do anything you would be embarrassed to see on the front page of the newspaper."* This is extraordinarily good advice. Doing something that is unethical, immoral, or worst of all illegal may be expedient in the short run. However, in the long run, the truth always emerges about the type of person you are. Inevitably, those kinds of actions will lead to major problems at work, at home, or could land you in jail.

Some of the most dramatic and high profile examples of this can be found in the business of professional sports. Pete Rose (baseball gambling), Barry Bonds (steroid usage), or Tiger Woods (serial infidelity), are just a few of the superstars who have screwed up their lives which should have been filled only with accomplishment, satisfaction, and happiness. It is likely your reaction to these stories is to think, "*What an idiot!*" Well, now that you are—or are about to become—a professional, you should not do the kind of things that if posted on the Internet people would say, "*What an idiot!*"

Hoops

A tragic example of someone not heeding Gary's advice was a client and good friend whom I will call Hoops. As a high school kid in New Jersey, Hoops was a big-time basketball star. When he became my client, he was in his late 30s and looked like he could still dunk. Hoops was handsome, tall, and lanky. When he walked, his arms and legs seemed to move independently, but because he was a great athlete the overall effect was not a cacophony of movement but rather a symphony of coordination. Also, I knew Hoops was a great athlete because within a year of taking up golf, he became a single-digit handicapper.

Depending on how active the market is, a bond salesperson might be on the phone with his largest accounts as often as 20 or more times a day. This is especially true for U.S. Treasuries, which are the largest and most liquid part of the bond market. Given that degree of interaction, it is not unusual for Wall Street salespeople to become very friendly with their clients, and during my career I was lucky to have a number of clients become my good friends.

One of the highlights of each workday was my first call to Hoops in the morning. He would pick up the phone and in a purposefully comical baritone say, "*Benjee...how are ya?*" The way Hoops greeted me conveyed how happy he was I called, and that was definitely *not* the kind of greeting clients generally gave to their Wall Street salespeople. This isn't because most clients were thoughtless or rude; it's that most clients are overwhelmed each day with salespeople, from literally dozens of Wall Street firms, trying to sell them stocks or bonds. This, combined with the enormous pressure to make money trading, is why most clients often do not look forward to talking to their Wall Street salespeople—even the ones they like. I understood this dynamic well and it is one of the reasons I appreciated and highly valued my relationship with Hoops.

I started covering Hoops when I was at Morgan Stanley in 1986 and continued to cover him when I went to Greenwich Capital. Hoops was not only a good and active client, but he also took it upon himself to teach me what he knew about the bond business. He was a proprietary trader for one of the largest commodity firms in the world, and his particular expertise was buying Treasury bonds he thought were cheap and selling Treasury bonds he thought were expensive. This is called relative value arbitrage and this business was a good fit for Greenwich Capital because we were known as one of the very best relative value trading firms in the Treasury market.

While most Wall Street salesmen go through some kind of formal training program, the only way to really learn the business is on the job. As a junior salesman at Bankers Trust, as a mid-level salesman at Morgan Stanley, and as a senior salesman at Greenwich Capital, I learned a great deal about the bond market from my co-workers and an equal amount from my clients. More than any other client, Hoops was incredibly helpful and generous with his time, explaining how he looked at the market generally and his individual trades specifically.

By the early 1990s, Hoops was one of the largest and most profitable Treasury clients on Wall Street. He was making a very good living and had a great deal of autonomy to run his business. He seemed to appreciate his good fortune and never acted entitled. I admired Hoops and looked up to him as someone to emulate.

Just as it looked like Hoops was going to be a perennial all star, he got thrown out of the game: he was caught not playing by the rules. A salesman from another Wall Street firm conspired with Hoops to kickback a portion of his commissions to Hoops in return for his business. The story got even weirder because the only reason this scheme came to light was the other salesman's phone was being tapped by the FBI. It turned out this salesman was a real bad guy and was being investigated for his role in an insurance scam which involved killing horses to collect insurance money. Hoops, of course, knew nothing about the insurance scam, but he was involved in the kickback scheme that was uncovered during the FBI investigation.

While in no way condoning or trying to justify what Hoops did, in fairness, his illegal act should be put into perspective. Looked at one way, what Hoops did was to negotiate a discount price for his transactions. The Bad Guy's firm was paying the same amount to The Bad Guy for Hoops' business—The Bad Guy simply was splitting his commissions with Hoops. This made it less expensive for Hoops to trade with that firm.

The problem was neither The Bad Guy nor Hoops disclosed this arrangement to their respective firms. Since Hoops was a proprietary trader and paid a percentage of his profit and losses, any additional revenue he generated through this commission splitting agreement should have been shared with the commodity firm.

Hoops paid a terrible price for his transgression. He lost his job and all his savings in legal costs and fines, and was banned by the SEC from the securities business for a number of years. After being on top of the world, Hoops crashed and burned. He was flat broke, his wife left him, and he was never able to get back on his feet again because, even after his SEC ban was completed, nobody would hire him. When he legally could go back to work in the industry, I tried my best to get Hoops a job at Greenwich Capital, but I met with such fierce resistance from my legal department that I finally gave up. Our chief legal counsel kept asking me, *"With all the other candidates out there, why would we even consider hiring this guy?"*

Hoops stayed in touch with me for many years, but the news on his career and life never got any better. At one point he became a one-man wine wholesaler and I filled my basement with 50 identical cases of white wine he needed to sell. It took me a year to drink some of it and I gave the rest away. The next time I heard from Hoops he asked me to pay him up front for a large shipment of wine he would deliver to me. I gave him the money, but the wine never arrived. I wasn't angry; the whole thing just made me sad.

Three Lessons from Hoops:

1. It takes a lifetime to build a reputation and a single act can destroy it. Most mistakes can be corrected and don't do lasting damage to a person's reputation or career. Some things, however, cannot be undone and, unfortunately for Hoops, his transgression was one of them.

2. If you are fortunate to find yourself in a senior position in a large organization, there will be instances when you can do things to help friends. Blue was a perfect example of this. Hiring Blue helped him, helped me, and, most importantly, helped Greenwich Capital. In the case of Hoops, however, it would have been wrong for me to overrule our chief legal counsel. This issue goes to the heart of a manager's relationship with his employer. When you become a manager, your job is to serve the interests of the company—not to use the company to serve your interests.

3. If you are fortunate enough to have a friend like Hoops as
   a client, count your blessings. Hope that he remains your
   customer for a very long time because you will miss him when
   he's gone.

THE GOOD, THE BAD, AND THE UGLY

The most memorable salesman I ever worked with was a guy whom
we called Big Hank because he was physically large—and his personality was *enormous*.

Big Hank

My first memory of Big Hank was the day he called me out of the
blue and said he wanted to discuss coming to work at Greenwich
Capital as a salesman. At the time, I was covering accounts as well
as being the sales manager, and I remember being a little short with
Big Hank because I was extremely busy and I never heard of him. I
forget exactly what I said, but it was something like "*Send me your
resume and I'll take a look.*" As I was about hang up, I heard Big Hank,
like a policeman shouting "*Drop that gun*," bellow, "*HEY…DON'T
HANG UP! YOU WANT TO TALK TO ME!*"

You might think I would be put off by a job seeker yelling at me,
but like an expert fisherman, Big Hank set the hook deep, and suddenly I was no longer busy. I was all ears because I had to know who
this guy was and why he thought I needed to talk to him. Big Hank
then gave me an aggressive sales pitch on how he was an outstanding
salesman from one of the smaller U.S. Treasury firms and was looking to move.

Soon after finishing that memorable first conversation with
Big Hank, I called a few of his customers and learned, as advertised,

he was an outstanding salesman who covered a number of large accounts in continental Europe. Aside from being fearless, as he displayed on his cold call to me, Big Hank was a one-man, three-ring circus. He was legendary throughout Europe for his positively insane business trips. The stories of Big Hank's outrageous trips always involved some combination of him drinking to excess, throwing up multiple times, doing himself or others bodily harm, and, much like Sherman's march through Georgia, leaving a wake of destruction in his path.

On these trips, Big Hank was also famous for missing his daytime business meetings or, if he did show up at his client's office, he looked as if he had just survived a war and reeked of alcohol and general debauchery. This is because Big Hank was far too busy getting smashed, or too busy being passed out, to have time to waste showering and changing—and his clients wouldn't have it any other way! After I hired Big Hank, clients throughout Europe lined up to do business with Greenwich Capital in hopes he would put them on his schedule for his next business trip, so afterward they would have fresh Big Hank material to entertain their friends. Unfortunately, Big Hank's craziness was not confined to business trips.

The Big Hitter Strikes Out

As a major Treasury bond dealer, Greenwich Capital did hundreds, if not thousands, of transactions with clients each day. Mistakes were inevitable and considered to be a routine though unpleasant fact of life. However, nothing about Big Hank was routine. Apparently, he was not satisfied with making garden variety errors. One day, Big Hank took a buy order from his client and, rather than immediately giving it to our traders (which was the *only* way business was *ever* transacted), he told no one about this order. Why would Big Hank break every rule in the book and pull this crazy stunt? Knowing him well I believe there were two reasons:

- First, Big Hank relished living up to his larger-than-life reputation and if the market went down he could buy the bonds for his clients at a cheaper price and be a hero.

- Second, by "holding" this buy order, if the market went down and our traders could buy his clients' bonds below the level of the order, Big Hank could "mark up" the bonds and make more money for himself.

There was just one catch: for these things to occur the market needed to move lower. Well, the market did move, but it moved straight up and the losses started climbing like a thermometer in July! Big Hank panicked and, rather than owning up to what he had done, went home that evening accompanied by a terrible secret: Greenwich Capital owed his client these bonds, and it would now cost a few hundred thousand dollars more for Greenwich to buy the bonds than when Big Hank was given the order by his client.

As always seems the case, time passing makes errors worse, and by the next morning, the market had jumped up more. When Big Hank finally came clean and revealed his sad story, and our traders "covered" the trade by buying the client's bonds, Greenwich Capital was out $1 million!

This extraordinary tale reached me less than a minute after Big Hank confessed and I immediately called him into my office. At this point, he was not his blustery self; he was shaken and defeated. Big Hank well understood he was responsible for a colossal and inexcusable error and there was going to be a price to pay. The only question was what that price would be.

With Big Hank sitting across from my desk, I found myself at a loss for words. What he had done was so outrageous, I didn't know what to say. After a few seconds of silence, the best I could muster was, "*What the hell were you thinking?*" For the first time in this saga, Big Hank did something intelligent. He didn't try to explain and he simply threw himself on the mercy of the court. I seriously considered firing Big Hank on the spot. However, looking at him, I was certain he would never do anything remotely similar again. Also, I liked Big Hank and didn't want to lose his sales production, so I searched for another punishment.

For starters, I told Big Hank he was *on probation*—whatever that meant. There was no such thing as probation at Greenwich Capital, but it sounded good. The second part was a very real punishment: Big Hank would have to pay back every penny of the $1 million loss out of his own pocket. Even for a big hitter like Big Hank this was a huge amount of money, but he didn't argue. Then I told Big Hank to get out of my sight.

In case you're wondering just how crazy Big Hank really was and just how stupid I am, let me answer both questions with one word: very. Within a year, after he had paid the firm back in full, Big Hank again intentionally mishandled a client order. Although this time there was no financial loss to the firm, I nevertheless had no choice but to fire Big Hank, and he lumbered out the door of Greenwich Capital for the last time—gone but not forgotten.

Three Lessons from Big Hank:

1. Being a fearless salesperson is a rare and valuable talent, and if you have it, or are able to develop it, you will succeed in sales. Being fearless means never worrying about being rejected. If you can be fearless you greatly increase your chances to succeed because you will try to make more sales (because you don't fear rejection), and you will be rejected less often (because many people respond positively to confidence). Also, people enjoy being entertained. While Big Hank had an extreme style of entertainment (and one I don't recommend), the best salesmen, one way or another, work hard to keep their clients happy.

2. The mission of *The Bigs* is to tell you what works and what doesn't work, in the real world. This book is not about the way things should be—it's about the way things are. In the real world there is often a different set of rules for stars, and Big Hank was a star. However, if you're not yet a star it is highly unlikely your manager will bend over backwards to give you a second chance as I did for Big Hank.

3. This last lesson is as much about my screw up as it is about Big Hank's. Back then, I chose to focus on the fact Big Hank often acted insanely (which, like his clients, I marveled at), and he was trying to get the bonds for his client at a better price to be a hero. In retrospect, I believe Big Hank's actions, first and foremost, were for personal gain. This showed a lack of integrity on his part which was inexcusable and he should have been fired immediately. The lesson for you as an employee is to *always* act with personal and professional integrity and as a manager to *always* insist on integrity from your employees. For this issue there should be no exceptions and no second chances—not even for stars.

BREAKING THE GOLDEN RULE

It will come as no surprise to people who know me (especially Leigh!) that I make mistakes—plenty of them. Even for me, however, the following story displays breath-taking stupidity. *My Golden Rule for how to conduct yourself at work is to never say anything negative about anybody in your office.* Sharing this story is painful because I made a total mess of this situation and there was no one to blame but me.

The two largest front office departments of Greenwich Capital—the U.S. Treasury and Mortgage departments—always had a friendly rivalry. This was not surprising given they were similar businesses, staffed with similar highly competitive people, sitting side by side. However, in business as in sports, it doesn't take much to transform a friendly rivalry into a not-so-friendly feud.

The Minister

When I became sales manager for Treasuries, the sales manager for Mortgages was someone I will call The Minister because, after he left Greenwich Capital, he graduated from divinity school. We should have been friends. We were the same age, shared friends outside of work, and we both loved Greenwich Capital. However, given the competition between the two departments, The Minister and I always had a somewhat chilly relationship. What turned that chill into a deep-freeze was my stupidity.

In 1996, on a business trip with a senior Greenwich Capital mortgage salesman, I let my guard down and confessed to my travel companion that I didn't like The Minister much. I may have been a little more colorful than that, but the truth is I did not have any good reason to not like him. By this point, I had broken at least two of my bedrock principles. I had previously allowed my relationship with a co-worker (The Minister) to devolve into a poor one, and, even worse, I had just broken my Golden Rule: *Never speak ill of someone assuming it won't get back to him.*

Unbeknownst to me, my indiscretion quickly did get back to The Minister and over the next two years our previously tenuous relationship further deteriorated. It so happened, at that time, Ted, Chip, and Gary needed help running Greenwich Capital and they wanted The Minister and me to become Co-Chief Operating Officers—a huge promotion for both of us. They decided, however, to not do it because it was obvious The Minister and I could not work together.

Finally, a mutual friend informed me The Minister had been told of my hostile comments two years prior. I asked The Minister to dinner and apologized. The Minister, understanding it was in the firm's and our personal interests to bury the hatchet, reached across the table, and as he shook my hand said, "*You're not as dumb as you look.*" (While no great compliment, I guess I had progressed from my college campus interview with J.P. Morgan when I *was* every bit as dumb as I looked.) The Minister and I almost immediately were given our promotions, and we became trusted partners and good friends as Co-COOs—and now we are back working together at CRT.

It is ironic this issue tripped me up so badly because I believe my normally rigorous adherence to my Golden Rule was a major reason, from early on, I was viewed as a leader at Greenwich Capital. I guess one could say the moral to the story is "All's well that ends well"—but the real lesson is to always follow the Golden Rule and never say anything negative about anybody in your company. To do otherwise is unprofessional, unnecessary, and more often than not will come back to haunt you.

IF YOU'RE LUCKY ENOUGH TO GET RICH ONCE

A few years ago, I was watching Jim Cramer, the hyperkinetic stock picker who has his own show, *Mad Money*, on CNBC. I believe the basic premise of his show (advising nonprofessional investors on which individual stocks to buy) is a bad idea for most people. However, Cramer is a very bright guy who has "been through the wars" and often has some valuable insights. On this particular show, Cramer screamed, "*If you're lucky enough to get rich once—don't blow it!*" My good friend at Greenwich Capital, The Knight, is a perfect example of Cramer's sound advice. On the surface, the story about The Knight appears to be about financial management. However, the most important lessons are much broader.

The Knight

The Knight graduated from college a year after me, and he went directly to Wall Street. When we met on the trading floor of Bankers Trust in 1983, he was already well on his way to becoming a star Treasury bond salesman. We quickly became friends and have remained close ever since. After Bankers Trust, The Knight worked at Salomon Brothers (while I was at Morgan Stanley), and in 1987, we both joined Greenwich Capital. While working at Salomon, The Knight married a lovely young woman who described her husband as, "*My knight in shining armor,*" and the way she said it you knew that is exactly how she felt about him.

The Knight grew up in a small town in Michigan and was one of nine children, four girls and five boys. The Knight's father, a strapping man whose handshake envelopes your hand as if he was wearing a boxing glove made of muscle, worked at Ford Motor Company for his entire career. The Knight and his four brothers lived in a single bedroom above the garage and, while I have never seen it, I always smile when I imagine that scene. All the boys were good athletes, but my friend was the best. A football, basketball, and baseball star in high school, The Knight attended the University of Pennsylvania where he was the starting quarterback for his sophomore, junior, and senior years.

In addition to be being a great athlete, The Knight had an engaging personality and loved to compete. In other words, he was an outstanding salesman. Clients liked him so much that even to this day when I run into clients who know both of us, after saying something perfunctory about how glad they are I'm still alive, I can tell the only question they really care about is: "*How's The Knight?*"

With the money he earned as a salesman, The Knight has been both smart and lucky as an individual investor. In 1996, he correctly identified the Internet as the next big thing and he made a substantial bet, but a bet he could afford to lose, on a start-up Internet company (that I'll call High Flyer). He made this investment as part of an informal consortium of six acquaintances who each invested an equal amount, and they all purchased stock at $1 per share. The other five members of the consortium were less financially successful, and less financially sophisticated, than The Knight. They were simply a group of young professionals in their 30s who saw an opportunity to invest in a business they believed in. The amount they each invested in this start- up was more than they could afford to lose, but they had an idea, combined with an opportunity, and went for it.

This set of facts (unsophisticated investors investing more than they should in a start-up company) almost never ends well. This time, however, it began spectacularly well. To their credit, the consortium nailed it and this company became one of the highest fliers of the dot-com boom, reaching a high of more than $200 a share in 1999.

By that time virtually *everyone* was blindly in love with Internet stocks. Wall Street analysts were projecting High Flyer's stock would continue climbing to over $1,000 a share! The consortium members were giddy with optimism. The Knight shared this optimism, and why not? High Flyer had already gone from $1 to $200 per share, and by December 1999 it had a market capitalization of almost $60 billion.* The Knight, however, was different than the other consortium members because he had a plan. His plan was to sell

*While the dot-com boom bestowed exorbitant valuations on most technology companies, High Flyer was one of a select few which went completely bananas. In the nine months prior to reaching its peak valuation, this four year old start-up reported total revenues of $15 mm and a net income loss of $6 mm. Nevertheless, in December 1999, the stock market deemed High Flyer to be more valuable than many established Internet heavyweights (such as AOL and Yahoo) as well as many "old economy" giants (such as GM and Gillette). The real name of High Flyer is Internet Capital Group (ticker: ICGE).

enough of his High Flyer stock so he would have sufficient money to comfortably take care of his family if he decided to retire to have fun with his wife and three children.

As The Knight was preparing to execute his plan to sell a good chunk of his High Flyer stock, he came under withering criticism from his consortium partners: "*Didn't he believe in this great company?… Shouldn't they all stick together?… Didn't he want to be a billionaire?*" The pressure put on The Knight was intense and included calls from the senior management of High Flyer (who were now considered virtual gods in the new dot-com world) urging him not to sell, and explaining why the best was yet to come for the company. The Knight, however, cared more about financially protecting his family than he did any dreams of grandeur. He stuck to his plan and sold the amount of his High Flyer stock (at astronomically high prices) he had previously determined was needed to achieve his goal of financial security. The other consortium members, who didn't have plans, stuck to their optimism and sold nothing. The next chapter in this saga was the stock of High Flyer, after climbing like a rocket from 1996 to 1999, fell like a stone and by 2001 was back to the $1 per share price where the wild ride began.

The epilogue to this story is The Knight retired in 2000, and for the next 10 years had the privilege of enjoying parenting and coaching his two daughters and son. Three years ago, with his youngest in high school and the other two out of college, The Knight decided to go back to work—not because he needed to, but because he wanted to. Happily for me, we are back together, this time at CRT Capital.

Two Lessons from The Knight's Tale:

1. While large investments in individual companies, especially start-ups, are generally a bad idea, there are exceptions to every rule. When you see an opportunity you believe in, you need

be ready and willing to act. However, these rule-breaking exceptions must be subjected to great scrutiny and handled with great discipline. The Knight did his homework researching High Flyer and its management, didn't invest more than he could afford to lose, and managed his investment like a pro. The Latin phrase *carpe diem*, or "seize the day," is a perfect description of The Knight's experience with High Flyer. At times, you need to seize the day if you want to reap significant rewards. However, the greater the risks the more thought and care you need to apply.

2. Few things worth doing are ever easy. Standing up for your beliefs can be a scary and lonely exercise. The Knight understood he *invested* in High Flyer; he hadn't married it. All the consortium members were free to sell—that decision was up to them. Since The Knight was the sole breadwinner, his family depended on him to protect them and he took that responsibility dead seriously. The Knight never got his loyalties confused, never got swept away in the insane emotions of the dot-com boom, and showed great discipline and fortitude in sticking to his plan of prioritizing his family's well-being above all else. In doing so, The Knight dug a deep moat and built high walls around the security and well-being of his wife and three children.

DON'T PICK FIGHTS YOU CAN'T WIN

Fighting in the office is a bad idea, period. It makes people unhappy, unproductive, and is a huge waste of time and energy. Also, even the winner often loses. This is because every boss wants his employees to get along, so rarely does anyone come out of the ring looking better than he did going in. Nevertheless, I realize serious disputes in the office are a fact of life for many people at some time during their careers. If you, for legitimate or illegitimate reasons, feel you need to fight—*only fight if you know with certainty you will win.*

Mr. Nuts

The most ridiculous example of someone not heeding this advice involved a veteran Wall Street trader and manager whom I will call Mr. Nuts. He had been at Greenwich Capital just over a year and had shown some promise. The problem was he could not get along with the other managers. The root causes of these conflicts were Mr. Nuts's extreme ambition and sledgehammer style of dealing with people. Sometimes I coached him and sometimes I let slide the problems he created.

Eventually, it seemed Mr. Nuts got bored fighting with the other managers and he turned on his one supporter at Greenwich—*me*! I started to hear snippets of conversations that didn't sound great, but I tried to ignore them hoping Mr. Nuts would get it together.

Finally, I got a report from an impeccable source that Mr. Nuts told a group of employees he expected to soon have *my* job. Well, that broke me, so it was time to break him. The next day I called Mr. Nuts into my office. If I could remember exactly what I said to him I would tell you, but it's lost in the fog of time. However, I do remember it was a quick meeting—and Mr. Nut's last ever at Greenwich Capital. I am still amazed that Mr. Nuts thought he could pick a fight with a CEO and get away with it.

In addition to the obvious "don't pick fights you can't win" lesson, there is another even more important lesson here. *While ambition is a great thing, your #1 focus must always be on doing a great job. Great performance, not great ambition, is the foundation of all great careers.* Looking at my own career, if I had been singularly focused on becoming the CEO of Greenwich Capital, I believe *I* would have gone nuts. The likelihood of me becoming CEO waxed and waned as the fortunes of my career went up and down, as the performance of others went up and down, and as the ownership of Greenwich Capital changed hands three times. Mr. Nuts lived up to his name not only by picking a fight with a CEO, but also by allowing his ambition to run wildly ahead of his performance.

NEVER BE LIKE NEVER

The last story in this chapter is about a young woman, I'm calling Never, who joined Greenwich Capital a few years before Jay and I took over as Co-CEOs. From the first day she walked in the door, Never projected an aura of confidence and competence which was evident to all. Being young, Never did not have a senior position at the company. However, because she handled every task given to her efficiently and professionally, more responsibility naturally flowed her way. Never quickly made many friends and was liked and respected throughout the firm.

Your first few years at a company are about establishing a foundation on which to build a successful career. The foundation Never constructed in her first few years at Greenwich Capital was rock solid, but then cracks began to appear in that seemly perfect foundation. The first crack was so small it was not really regarded as a problem but more as a surprising personality quirk. Almost simultaneously, a handful of employees who worked closely with Never realized she *never* took responsibility for any mistakes and *never* apologized for anything. It had taken a few years to notice this because Never was so good at her job she did not make many mistakes. Never was human, however, and did make some.

When co-workers realized she never took responsibility for her mistakes, it became a source of aggravation since Greenwich Capital was a collegial working environment where taking responsibility for your actions was the norm. Because Never was well liked, competent, and hard working, people did not dwell on this issue and instead viewed it as a peccadillo which was assigned to the "nobody's perfect" bin.

The problem was, over the following few years, new and much more serious cracks in the foundation appeared as Never began to periodically abuse her position of power. While she still didn't find fault with herself, she was quick to find it in others and in subtle, and not so subtle, ways let them know. While there were numerous examples of Never's abuse of power, the worst was her treatment of one poor guy in the mailroom. The Poor Guy was in his mid-40s and a gentle soul who loved working at Greenwich Capital. A senior manager of the firm complained he was not receiving his daily newspaper delivery to his office. Never, doing her best Captain Queeg imitation, immediately confronted The Poor Guy and accused him of stealing the newspapers and told him she was going to see he got fired. To say he was distraught would be a gross understatement. The world he loved was crashing down around him.

Never got the Head of Facilities involved since the mailroom reported to him. Before he agreed to fire anybody, he decided to look at security tapes to see what really happened to the newspapers in question. Low and behold, the tapes confirmed the master criminal was a very senior and very powerful trader at the firm. Since the infraction was so minor (and the trader so major) the punishment meted out to him was he was politely asked to stop taking the newspapers.

The worst part of the story is when Never was informed of the truth, she laughed it off as if it was a big joke and, of course, *never* apologized to The Poor Guy. As you would expect, the goodwill and support Never had rightfully earned over the preceding years started to disappear. When Never left Greenwich, eight years after her arrival, it was sad to realize most of her co-workers were more relieved than sorry to see her go.

Three Lessons from Never:

1. Take responsibility for all mistakes you make and, if you are a competent and valued employee, when you do take

responsibility it will be viewed as a sign of strength, not weakness, by your co-workers.

2. Understand that how your boss views you will be largely a function of how your peers and subordinates see you. All my interactions with Never, from her first day at Greenwich Capital to her last, were nothing but positive. However, my opinion of her deteriorated as I came to understand how she treated her peers and subordinates.

3. The initial warm reception that Never received at Greenwich Capital is not unusual. You should appreciate that most employees are anxious to embrace smart and hard working new co-workers. Everyone starts each new job (especially their first job) with a sense of trepidation; "*Will I fit in?*" or, "*Will people be nice to me?*" The truth is most people at most companies love having new employees join who are hard working, pleasant, and have the ability to help make the company better. As with so many other issues, work and sports are identical this way. If you are a rookie and helping the team win, and are supportive and considerate of your teammates, you will be welcomed with open arms and held in high regard.

Chapter 5

Living a Happy Life

Happiness and the life you experience can be a virtuous circle. A happy person has a better chance of experiencing a full and productive life because people are drawn to happiness like politicians to a microphone. If you are happy, people are going to want to work with and for you—which is a great starting point for any career.

THE SECRET

Quite surprisingly, at a corporate golf outing 25 years ago, I learned a secret that changed my life. After cocktails, there was a speech by the famous basketball coach, Rick Pitino, who had just been hired by the Boston Celtics. That year, the Celtics had the good fortune of owning the rights to draft two of the first seven eligible college players. The NBA draft was structured so there was a lottery to decide the order of the first seven lottery picks. Coach Pitino was excited; in the best case, he would be able to draft the #1 and #2 best players available. What happened instead, by luck of the draw, the Celtics drew the #6 and #7 picks—an unmitigated disaster!

You can imagine how Coach Pitino felt. This devastating blow was likely to have enormous negative consequences for the Celtics, and the coach personally, for years to come. Coach Pitino relayed this story not to elicit sympathy, but rather to tell the audience what happened next. I remember every word he spoke:

> The next day, a reporter called and asked me if I was upset by the terrible bad luck of getting the worst two lottery picks. I told him the truth. Yes, I had been very upset, but then I told him something else which was true. Five minutes after I heard the news, I realized nobody was forcing me to be upset, and I made the conscious decision to *choose to not be upset.* Instead, I decided to channel my energy into making the #6 and #7 picks *I did have* better than the #1 and #2 picks *I didn't have.* Immediately, I was no longer upset. I was now focused and determined.

Well, this thought blew my mind and was like a slap across the face. The idea my happiness was *totally in my hands* was an entirely new concept for me. From that moment on, I committed myself to choosing to be happy. I hadn't been a miserable person before, but this new approach simplified my life greatly. Whenever challenges or problems came along, I no longer had to decide if I would be upset. I knew in advance the answer was no.

The Rude Waiter

I have a great fondness for the Rick Pitino story because it changed my life in a very positive way. However, it is a story about a NBA head coach dealing with a situation only a handful of people will ever encounter. A commonplace example of happiness being a choice is when you receive poor service at a restaurant because the waiter is rude or inattentive. This happens to all of us on occasion; but, the way people react is indicative of how they respond to other challenges—big or small. Sometimes people become furious, sometimes they suffer in silence, but most often their reaction is somewhere in between. Since embracing Coach Pitino's philosophy that happiness is a choice, I behave differently than I used to.

Now, I am unwilling to *ever* allow poor service to spoil my dinner. I may not go back to a restaurant, but I will not permit a

rude waiter to ruin my evening. I take this thought process to such
an extreme that even when I don't receive good service, I still leave
a full tip. I understand a poor tip is a sign of displeasure and, since
I have not allowed myself to be upset by the poor service, I don't feel
it necessary to leave a poor tip. That may sound a little crazy, but
it's simply a reflection of my determination to not allow people or
situations I don't control to make me unhappy.

If it sounds like I'm soft when it comes to dealing with waiters
and waitresses, that would also be true. Having worked summers as a
waiter and busboy, I have great empathy for those jobs—particularly
at busy restaurants such as the two I worked at in Newport, Rhode
Island. However, when I receive bad service my attitude of refusing
to even acknowledge it is really quite selfish. If I engage and get
annoyed, or start telling the waiter how to do his job, then I have
become involved in his problem and I have no interest in that.

The Dogs and The Button

Ivan Pavlov was a Russian physiologist who won the 1904 Nobel
Prize in Physiology or Medicine for his groundbreaking research
into "conditioned reflexes." He was most famous for his work with
"Pavlov's dogs." He discovered if he sounded a bell when he fed
his dogs, they would begin to salivate. After he repeated this a few
times, he found that his dogs would begin to salivate when the bell
rung—even if no food was presented to them. This kind of learned
involuntary reaction is now referred to as a Pavlovian response.

Whenever I go to a restaurant, I understand there is a risk of
receiving poor service and, as you now know, I am mentally prepared
not to let that upset me. However, occasionally, I still get angry and
it is almost always something I dislike that happens unexpectedly.
Like most everyone, I feel an immediate, and sometimes intense,
flash of anger. But, the next thought that comes into my mind is
"*I'm losing.*" This is because one of my highest goals is to be happy,

and if I'm angry clearly I am not accomplishing this goal. Being a competitive person, I don't like to lose so my immediate response to anger is to do whatever it takes in that situation to hit my Emotional Reset Button and start again. Looking for that Button has become an instinctive, almost Pavlovian, response. Sometimes I can find The Button more easily than others, however, I always try to locate it, and hit it, as quickly as possible.

One of the great things about The Button is the immediate feedback. If I think I hit The Button, but I'm still angry, I know I missed the mark. I keep searching until I find it and hit it squarely. This is never a long drawn-out process. Like Pavlov's Dog's strong desire for food, I have a strong desire to be happy, so now it rarely takes me more than a minute to overcome my knee-jerk reaction of anger and move on to a happier state of mind.

CREATING A HAPPY LIFE

Choosing to be happy (as illustrated by Coach Pitino, the The Rude Waiter, and The Button) is an important step to happiness. *However, these examples better describe how to not be unhappy, rather than how to be happy.* To be consistently happy, I believe you need to *create* a life which makes you feel good about yourself. This is not easy and it takes maturity, self-awareness, hard work, and intelligence. You must decide what makes you happy and then go for it.

Prioritizing Happiness

When I arrived on the Bankers Trust trading floor in 1983, the head of the Treasury bond business was a gentleman named Alan Rogers. Despite his senior role, Alan always took the time to speak to the junior people on the trading floor. While he gave us a great deal of good advice, what I remember best was when he said, "*It is impossible to accomplish anything of real value unless you first make it a priority and believe you can achieve it.*" Surprisingly, it is often difficult to get people to embrace happiness as a goal. They are often so focused on other goals the idea of prioritizing their happiness seems somehow irrelevant or self-indulgent. Look at it this way: If you were a parent and given a choice for your children to be either more happy, or more successful, which would you choose? I happen to know the answer because I have asked many people this question many times. All people choose more happiness over more success for their children. So why shouldn't you prioritize happiness the same way in your life?

I have never seen an unhappy person become happy because of what he achieved professionally. Successful people certainly get enjoyment from achieving their goals, but that pleasure is invariably fleeting. The people I know who are happy are that way because of a predisposition towards happiness and how they conduct their personal relationships. It's never solely about what they accomplish professionally.

Life's Bigs and Littles

After having almost died and going through seven major aortic surgeries, many times I have had friends and acquaintances say to me "*With all you've been through, it must make you focus on what's important in life.*" I do think my health episodes helped me gain perspective. However, what I have learned is, in some ways, diametrically opposite of what people expect. When they make that statement, most people believe I must spend more time thinking about my health, my family, or other big issues. While that is true, it also has made me value the little issues more.

When I arrived home from the hospital after my second surgery in 1994, I found myself in a mental state I had never experienced and it frightened me. As I was recuperating, I realized all the little things I used to care about no longer were important to me: the Yankees, reading Page Six of the *New York Post*, what we were having for dinner, and so on. These issues, and all the other little issues I used to care about, no longer held any interest for me; they all now seemed preposterously unimportant.

Fortunately, this emotional state was not as overwhelming as the blackness I briefly experienced after my first surgery, but it lasted much longer (almost a week) and I was beginning to fear it would be my "new normal." Happily, this mental state eventually evaporated and I gratefully returned to my old self—able to care passionately about many little things.

This episode transformed the way I feel about the little things. While I used to think my mild obsession with professional sports was a waste of time, I now view it as good thing because it gives me pleasure. (Though I am still trying to convince Leigh of its merits!) I look at the interests of others, especially my children, the same way. I care less about *what* they care about than that their lives are full of things, big *and* little, that bring them happiness.

Health and Happiness

I have never forgotten a comment I read many years ago from a psychiatrist. He said, "*Before I take on any new patients, I require them to go out and run or walk five miles and then come talk to me.*" His point was physical exercise and mental health are so intertwined that if you feel good physically you have a much better chance of feeling good mentally. I am convinced that psychiatrist was correct.

Happiness and Marriage

When people hear a relative or friend of theirs is going to get married, and they don't know the other person, typically the first questions they ask are, "*Is this new person well educated? Successful?*

Nice? Attractive?" If someone really cares about the prospects of the marriage, I think they should be asking: *"Is this friend's fiancé fundamentally happy?"* If the answer is *"yes,"* then the odds of a successful marriage are high. If the answer is *"no,"* then no matter how beautiful, well-educated, successful, or even nice the new person is there is reason to worry. While I generally avoid giving advice on affairs of the heart, in this case I am making an exception. Whatever qualities you look for in a spouse, please include "a happy person" at or near the top of your list. *Given the importance of the topic, this could be the single most valuable piece of advice you take away from* The Bigs.

MONEY AND HAPPINESS

You may wonder: "How does financial success relate to happiness?" A quick and undoubtedly true answer is, "It depends on the person." However, that isn't particularly helpful or illuminating. More useful are the results of a study, based on a Gallup survey of 450,000 Americans in 2008 and 2009, that revealed a surprising finding. This study concluded the "day-to-day contentment," or emotional well-being, of Americans went up as their income rose. However, at an income of $75,000 per year, increases in happiness plateaued. Above $75,000, while respondents could buy more stuff, that stuff did not lead to an increase in their happiness.

Due to cost of living disparities, having a $75,000 income is different in Manhattan than Montana. However, the important point this study makes is it does not take an ungodly amount of money to live a happy life (and having an ungodly amount of money probably will not make you any happier).

When it comes to the amount of financial and nonfinancial things you have, the only certain way these things can make you happy is if you feel fortunate to have them. We all know people who "have it all"—intelligence, good looks, good health, a loving family, plenty of money—yet they are still not happy. This is because they don't appreciate what they have. On the other hand, we all know people who have very little, however, they are happy because they feel lucky with what they do have. I am *not* arguing against ambition. We live in a competitive world and it's fun to compete. It simply means that while you are looking towards the future, and the goals you hope to accomplish, you need to appreciate the blessings you have today. *This* is the real secret of happiness. While most people intellectually know this "secret," few put much thought or effort into acting upon it. *Just like choosing to be happy, you can choose to appreciate what you have. If I could give one gift to those I love the most, it would be for them to always appreciate what they have.*

LEAVE YOUR BAGGAGE AT HOME

Everyone accumulates a certain amount of psychological baggage during their childhood. If you had a happy childhood, what you carry around is likely to be lighter than if your childhood was unhappy, but regardless, everyone carries around some baggage. The source is sometimes easily identified—someone, some group, or some event, did you wrong. However, more often, the source is murky.

Despite having a modestly unconventional upbringing from moving so many times, I believe my teenage baggage was about as conventional as it gets. It consisted of a low-level, but ever-present, insecurity towards others who were smarter, better looking, or more popular than I. Unfortunately, this was a very large group of people. This, combined with my rebellious attitude towards authority, gave me the bad attitude that got me virtually run out of my high school by irate coaches.

What snapped me out of my bad attitude, or stated differently, what got me to leave my baggage behind, was going to Hotchkiss.

The culture shock of leaving a second-tier high school for a first-tier boarding school was so dramatic it changed my outlook immediately. The demands of Hotchkiss were such you either got with the program or went home.

Again, my experiences in high school and boarding school were modestly unconventional. You may not yet have had a shock dramatic enough to make you drop your childhood baggage. *However, you need to appreciate how stunningly different the real world is from your previous life as a student and seize this moment to make a fresh start.*

The real world is so competitive you need *all* your focus and energy to choose, get, and do a great job. The insecurities and resentments from your childhood will just slow you down or, in some cases, sabotage your plans entirely. You are now a full grown man or woman and it is time to stand up, take responsibility, and start building the life you want to live.

The logical question is, *"How can I leave the past behind? It's been a part of me for so long."* The answer is identical to choosing to be happy or hitting your emotional reset button. You own the baggage and therefore you have the power to do whatever you want with it. My advice is decide to get rid of it *right now.* My expression for leaving the past behind is "traveling light." If you choose to travel light, I promise you will be more successful, and have more fun, than if you insist on lugging your baggage around.

A FINAL THOUGHT ON HAPPINESS

One reason people are unhappy is because they believe they should be more happy. While this might sound like a strange "through the looking glass" type of problem, it is actually very common, and it increases with age as people become more introspective about their lives. While I don't have a silver bullet to solve this vexing problem,

I do have a thought you might find reassuring: How happy you feel is partially determined by nature and partially by nurture. Some people are simply born more, or less, happy than others. Therefore, if you aren't blissfully happy all the time, it doesn't mean you are failing. It is likely at least part of your perceived lack of happiness is genetic.

Scientific studies have used adult twins, separated at birth, to examine this issue. In a typical case, one twin lived a life filled with all the good stuff: a loving family, achievement, financial security, and so on. The other twin lived a life with much less of the good stuff. However, from looking at the electrical waves in the areas of their brains which control happiness, as well as observing the twins and asking them about their perceived level of happiness, these studies found that twins separated at birth regularly displayed quite similar levels of happiness. The general consensus of these studies is, on aver-age, approximately half of people's level of happiness is determined by genetics.

If we accept these studies and their conclusions, so what? If happiness is significantly determined by genetics, what can we do about it? One way to look at this is similar to a genetic predisposition to being overweight. Through extra attention to diet and exercise this predisposition can be partially, or even fully, overcome. Also, accepting that genetics play a significant role in happiness can allow you to give yourself a break and not beat yourself up about not being happier. It really is a tragedy of self-flagellation to make yourself additionally unhappy because you feel your level of happiness is inadequate. Treasure the happiness you have, work hard to create more happiness for yourself and the ones you love, and don't allow anything you control (including insecurities about your level of happiness) to rob you of any of this *most* precious commodity.

A Self-Assessment

I would like to be able to tell you I walk around all day every day with a big smile on my face because I make it a priority to choose to be happy. However, that is not the case. As I think about the people I have known, I would guess my genetic predisposition for being happy is just about average. But whatever my baseline of happiness is, I know by choosing to be happy I have been able to move the needle in the right direction and I will always keep trying to push that needle.

Part Two

How to Choose, Get, and Do a Great Job

Introduction

Your Big League Career

Part Two is the specific information and advice you need to choose, get, and do a great job—as well as the critically important information of how to manage your finances. For many of you, this information and advice is why you picked up *The Bigs*. This is especially true for students in college and graduate school because for you *nothing* is (and nothing should be) more important than understanding how to choose a career, get a great job, and do a great job.

In the next three chapters, I will tell you exactly what you need to know to launch (or relaunch) your big league career.

Chapter 6

How to Choose Your Career

There is no magic formula to use, or treasure map to follow, which will lead you to find your ideal job and career. Many of you will learn the way I did: through trial and error. Therefore, since it is unlikely your first job/career choice will be your last, the most important thing is to dive into the pool of the working world and start swimming. However, it is a great advantage to get started on the best career path as soon as possible and that is what Chapter 6 will help you accomplish.

FOCUS ON WHAT YOU DO WELL

Since the real world is so competitive, you should spend less time trying to decide what you *want* to do and more time considering what you are *able* to do. Specifically, what you are able to do well enough that employers will want to hire you and provide you exciting career opportunities in the future. This means being honest with yourself about what your talents are and finding a job that matches up well with them.

Though I started my Wall Street career in sales, I always believed I could be a good trader. As you know, subsequent facts disabused me of that notion. After my failure as a trader, I was seriously being considered for, and I seriously considered taking, the job of chief financial officer of Greenwich Capital. What was I thinking? I was the guy who almost flunked accounting at Bankers Trust!

The truth is, I wasn't thinking—at least not rationally. It was my ego that didn't want me to go back to sales as a failure. It took almost dying from an aortic dissection to knock some sense into me and make me realize I should get back to doing something I was good at. Even if I had worked hard and done a respectable job as CFO, that position was never going to play to my strengths. Most importantly, it would have been nearly impossible for me to lead by example because I would have been heavily reliant on the finance department staff for technical expertise. In sales, however, doing what I was good at, I was able to be a true leader which was the catalyst for my future promotions.

Choosing a career you can do well, rather than doing what you want, might sound unappealing, but it isn't. The reason is the satisfaction you get from being good at your job. From my personal experiences, as well as observing family, friends, and co-workers, I know most professionals are most happy doing what they are good at.

SHOULD YOU FOLLOW YOUR PASSION

The most typical career advice you hear is to make your passion your career. Sometimes this is good advice, but often it isn't. My favorite example of when pursuing your passion may not be a good idea is if you *love* golf (and presumably are a good player). You might be tempted to become a golf professional, the kind who runs a country club course, not the kind who plays on the PGA tour (let's be honest, you're not *that* good).

If you become a golf professional because you love to play golf, you might be sorely disappointed. A golf pro spends 90% of his time in the pro shop selling shirts or out on the driving range trying, again, to teach Mrs. Jones how to get the ball in the air. You may find you actually play a lot less golf than you did before and you hate your job. However, if you decide to become a golf pro because you like the idea of running a small retail operation, you enjoy teaching, and are a naturally gregarious person, then being a golf pro could be your dream job.

Some people are so passionate about a topic or cause (e.g., sports, fashion, or the environment) their job must relate to that topic for them to be focused and energized. If you feel this way, then you absolutely should go with it. However, for many people, their passion may be best left as an outside interest to pursue in your free time. But you *do* need to find a career you are passionate about. I was extremely passionate about my career in finance, but I was never particularly passionate about finance itself. While I enjoyed learning how companies make money, and how markets work, my interest in those topics never approached passion. *What I was passionate about was competing in a competitive arena, being a contributor on a team, and supporting my family.*

CONSIDER YOUR LIFESTYLE

As you know, growing up, money was tight in my family and that was a constant source of tension. As I got older and understood more about money, our financial situation at times seemed downright scary. My mother was always conscious of the value of money, and she drilled into her children *"money gives you choices,"* which we often didn't have. Not surprisingly, I knew from a young age I wanted to make a good living, and I told my mother someday I would buy her a nice house and take care of her.

Despite the challenge of trying to divine the future, I urge you to be realistic about the long-term lifestyle effects many career choices entail. One factor to keep in mind is the significance of your career choice can vary greatly depending on where you choose to live.

For instance, living in a high cost area such as New York City on a schoolteacher's salary can be challenging. However, if you want to be a schoolteacher and live in a rural town in the Midwest, your lifestyle can be quite comfortable. Maybe you aren't the kind of person who cares much about material comfort and financial security. In that case your choices for careers are quite broad. If you do care, then your choices are more limited.

JOB SATISFACTION AND COMPENSATION

There are great reasons to pursue careers that provide modest compensation. Professionals such as teachers, firefighters, police officers, and healthcare workers serve as the backbone of our communities and often experience a great deal of job satisfaction and happiness. However, I believe there is a common misconception that if you strive to maximize your income it must be at the expense of job satisfaction and happiness.

My experience is that potentially lucrative careers can bring a great deal of job satisfaction. I know I laughed at least as much, and had at least as much fun, at work as I ever did in school. One reason is my co-workers and I were extremely focused on the task at hand and pressure is fertile ground for humor. Also, my co-workers generally got along quite well which was probably due to the competitive environment and because we shared common goals of wanting our company, our clients, and ourselves to prosper.

My mother began her career working in public relations for a hospital, took 12 years off to raise her five children, and then re-entered the working world as development director for two schools, a cathedral, and a college. She enjoyed her career which involved working with highly educated, capable, and idealistic people. However, because performance in non-profit organizations is not rewarded with compensation comparable to for-profits companies, competition in non-profits tends to focus on power and access which is a dynamic that can be toxic. My mother once told me, "*Just because someone is doing God's work does not mean he is a saint.*"

The truth of the matter is certain types of people are not indigenous to one industry and foreign to others. Virtuous, hard working, and competent people can be found just as easily in banking or law as in teaching or firefighting.

WALL STREET, THEN AND NOW

The purpose of *The Bigs* is not to promote one industry over another as a career path. Many of the stories I tell are from the world of finance because that was my primary career. However, due to my background, I am often asked the question, "*Is Wall Street still a good career path for me (or for my child)?*" I don't pretend to be unbiased, but for many people I would enthusiastically say, "*Yes!*" To me, Wall Street is just like all industries—only more so. More talking, more learning, more pressure, more winning, more losing, and potentially more compensation. I loved my Wall Street career, but it is true the business is changing.

To determine whether Wall Street is *still* a great place for careers (especially given the aftermath of the 2008 financial crisis), you need to understand that Wall Street is made up of many distinct businesses which each has its own drivers for profitability. But generally, Wall Street profits do well when the stock market does well, and we have seen an unprecedented growth in stock prices over the past three and a half decades.

Since 1980, the Dow Jones stock market index, including dividend reinvestment, has gone up in value more than 36 times! While stock prices are driven by many factors, one of the most powerful is interest rates. Investors can buy stocks—or bonds—and if interest rates on bonds go down (meaning you are being paid less money to own bonds), then stocks become relatively more attractive. Soon after I graduated from college in 1980, short-term interest rates peaked at 20% (today they are at 0%) and 30-year U.S. Treasury bonds peaked at over 15% (today they are under 4%). With this huge positive driver of stock prices behind us, and because of regulatory reform following the 2008 financial crisis, I don't think Wall Street will be quite as profitable, and therefore not quite as lucrative for employees, as it was prior to the crisis.

With that said, when I landed on the Bankers Trust trading floor in 1983, I vividly remember one of the veteran salesmen pulling me aside and explaining in great detail how the glory days of Wall Street had just ended. I remember thinking to myself, "*Darn it, just my luck to miss out on the good times!*" Today, there are again a lot of old guys singing the blues that the best days of Wall Street are behind us. Whether accurate or not, I believe the finance industry will continue to attract aggressive individuals who like a fast-paced and ever-changing environment. *For as long as we have free markets, Wall Street will continue to be an exciting place to work because it is shaped and driven by those often wild and crazy markets.* Also, compensation on Wall Street for top professionals will, I believe, continue to be substantially higher than for most other industries. The nature of the business is such that if you can do a slightly better job than the next person, it can be worth millions—or tens of millions—of dollars to your employer. Companies in *any* industry will always pay handsomely for the services of professionals who can deliver that kind of incremental revenue.

As with many industries, finance offers a huge variety of jobs and careers. It doesn't matter if your talents are in sales, quantitative analysis, writing, strategic thinking, leadership, or virtually anything else—there is a job in finance which will put your skills to work and to the test.

Chapter 7

How to Get a Great Job

Most college students realize they will have to work hard after they get a great job if they want to be successful. However, most students don't realize they should be prepared to work at least as hard to get that great job. *Getting a job is a job.* This is one of the many things I didn't understand when I began my job search. Expect your job search to be a long and challenging process. If it turns out to be short and easy, you can be pleasantly surprised.

YOU'VE GOT TO BE KIDDING

When young people ask me for advice on how to get a job, one of the first questions I ask is how many people they have contacted for interviews and how many people they intend to contact. Normally the answer is somewhere between 5 and 15. *That's crazy!* I tell young people they should prepare to contact *at least* 40 to 50 people in the industry of their choice. While they never say it to me out loud, I can see their eyes grow wider and I can almost hear them saying, "*You've got to be kidding!*" You may be thinking the same thing and also wondering if speaking to 40 to 50 people is really necessary.

It may take you fewer—or more—interviews, but this is a good number to plan for in order to conduct a professional job search which will give you the best chance of landing a great job.

Don't forget we are talking about an issue of vital importance which is worthy of all your attention and effort. Getting on the right career path, with the right job, will allow you to enjoy the time spent at work, which is critically important to your happiness. As long as your career lasts, it is likely you will be spending almost 40% of your waking hours at work (not to mention your commute and the time you spend thinking about work while you aren't at work). If that wasn't enough, the compensation from your job will determine much about your lifestyle as well as the freedom you have to pursue outside interests during the other 60% of the time your eyes are open.

None of this is meant to scare you. I mention it only so you appreciate that the importance of getting a great job is *more* than commensurate with the effort you need to be prepared to expend to get that job.

A GUIDE TO THIS CHAPTER

Since this chapter is a resource for you to refer back to, below is a guide which gives you an overview of the topics covered.

INFORMATIONAL AND JOB INTERVIEWS: SCORING GOALS

These two types of interviews are closely related but distinct. Informational interviews are granted as a favor by an interviewer to *help you* better understand an industry, company, or job. Job interviews are granted by an interviewer *so he* can find out if you are the best person to hire to fill a job opening.

If possible, it is always best to have in-person interviews. It is easier to make a strong, positive, impression in-person. Also, most job interviews are conducted face-to-face, so in-person informational interviews are good practice. If meeting in-person is not possible, substantive phone interviews also work, and I consider both in-person and phone interviews to count towards your goal of contacting 40 to 50 professionals. When you reach this goal, even if you haven't gotten a job yet, you will:

- Have learned enough about the industry to know if it's for you and what specific area appeals to you most.

- Have enough interviews to hone your sales skills and are able to explain why you are someone a company can't afford not to hire.

- Have enough "lines in the water" to hook and land a great job.

Scoring Goals

In your job search, as in sports, you need to focus on scoring the next goal and not worry about winning the game. You need to look at setting up each interview as scoring a goal. As long as your job search takes, each time you arrange an interview, or go on an interview, you should give yourself a high five! If you are learning, perfecting your sales skills, and putting lines in the water, you *are* winning. If you believe you only win when you get a job, then every day of your search, except the last, will be a loss. As in sports, losing begets losing, so don't allow yourself to be sucked into a downward spiral.

A job search can be a daunting and lonely exercise. With my daughter, Avery, I found it helpful for her to send me regular email updates of her progress (i.e., what interviews she arranged or experienced). This allowed me to periodically give her advice on the process and, most importantly, cheer loudly when she scored goals.

This mental approach is also valuable in your personal life. If you have 20 tasks to accomplish, but you can't get motivated to begin because the undertaking seems overwhelming, start by doing just one task and celebrating the completion of that task as a goal scored. Since it feels good to score a goal, you'll want to score another one. Before you know it, the game will be won and you will feel pretty darn good about yourself. A teacher once gave me this same advice when she said, "*the best way to get something done is to begin.*"

HOW TO GET INFORMATIONAL INTERVIEWS #1 *DEVELOPING YOUR NETWORK*

In the real world what is rewarded is both the ability to think creatively (not simply remember what you've been taught) and to have a network of strong professional relationships. When you are working, your relationships with subordinates, peers, bosses, and clients are all critically important to your success. *However, as important as relationships are in doing a great job, they are even more important in getting a great job.* Unless you have a rare skill, or an outrageously impressive resume, you need help from your network in order to get a great job.

As you begin to build your network, you will be surprised to realize you have *many* more potential professional contacts than you initially thought. Your contacts consist of almost every category of people you know personally and even more you don't yet know. These contacts are:

- Your family and their friends.
- Your friends and their friends.
- Industry contacts provided to you by the Career Services Office (CSO) at your college and the people these contacts are willing to introduce you to.
- Contacts obtained through professional social networking sites (primarily, LinkedIn).

HOW TO GET INFORMATIONAL INTERVIEWS #2 *USING YOUR NETWORK*

Many young people are shy and don't want to impose. However, you need to realize that everyone who ever had a job went through some version of what you are going through. Most people vividly remember *their* first job search and, therefore, are likely to help with yours. Finally, most people enjoy doing favors for others and, when the favor entails talking about themselves, they are normally more than happy to oblige.

In addition to being shy, another common mental straightjacket that limits the ability of many young adults to succeed is the attitude of, "I want to do this on my own." You need to understand that in business *nobody* does it on their own. Throughout your career, in an infinite variety of ways, you will depend on other people (and them on you). *As a college student or young professional you need to get with this program right now and, without embarrassment or false pride, develop and use all your contacts.*

Your Friends and Family

First, list all your friends and family who conceivably might have some ability to help you in your job search. This list should include *all* immediate and extended adult family members because you never know who they might know. For instance, you might want to get into advertising and your Uncle Fred is a fireman. While it may seem unlikely he can help you, it is possible that through playing weekend sports, coaching youth leagues, or some other activity or interest, Uncle Fred knows someone in advertising. Remember, you won't know who he knows unless you ask him.

This goes for all of your friends and family. Don't assume you know how they can help you. This advice particularly applies to those closest to you: parents, siblings, and close friends. These people are willing to move heaven and earth for you, but most of them will need to be told how they can help.

Your College Career Services Office

When I was a senior in college, the resources of Bowdoin's CSO were instrumental in getting my first job. First, The Head steered me into a great industry for my goals. Next, the CSO put me in touch with a dozen Bowdoin graduates in banking for informational interviews. By the time I had my interview with Superman, I had learned the basics about the business and learned how to sell myself in a professional context. Unless you were born with a silver spoon full of contacts in your chosen profession, you need to develop a *great* relationship with your CSO. How do you do this? Specifically, you need to befriend one or two influential individuals in the CSO. You do so by calling them by name, confiding in them your hopes and dreams, and generally wooing them into caring about you and your job search.

One of the easiest and most effective ways to establish a relationship with your college's CSO is to visit as early as possible (preferably during freshman year). Even if your college's CSO does not publicize that they provide individual counseling, you should still attempt to establish personal relationships within the CSO. It's human nature for CSO staffers to pay the most attention to students who have paid the most attention to them. Starting early will also give you a focus for your course selections as well as a focus for getting internships. The message here is that getting a great job is now too competitive to do as I did and wait until senior year. When talking to recent college graduates about their job search, the #1 regret I hear is, "I wish I started earlier." Visit your CSO as soon as possible.

The amount and quality of assistance you can expect to get from your college's CSO varies widely; some offer a good amount of personal attention and service to all students who come to them. At the other extreme, some CSOs will simply direct students to an alumni directory. Finally, some CSOs give a fair amount of personalized service to a small percentage of their students. If the latter is your college, your job is to sell yourself into that small percentage! If you are lucky enough to attend a college that attracts on-campus recruiting by companies in your chosen field, your CSO can be truly invaluable. The CSO can help you get job interviews and, in many cases, whisper in the ear of the recruiters which students the CSO thinks are winners.

The contacts you get from your CSO may be quite senior, quite junior, or somewhere in between. However, all are important to you in order to reach your initial goal of arranging at least 40 to 50 interviews. As you prioritize your contacts, when possible, you should schedule the junior professionals first and save the most senior ones for later when you know more about the industry, company, or job you most desire. Not surprisingly, the more senior a person is the more influential he can be in deciding who should be hired; therefore, you want to be fully on your game before you speak to contacts who have the most influence. It is also worth noting that the resources of CSOs are not only for current students, but are also available to alumni. Since few alumni avail themselves of the resources of the CSO, it is sometimes easier as an alum to stand out and get high quality attention from the staff.

HOW TO GET INFORMATIONAL INTERVIEWS #3 *ASKING FOR HELP*

Depending on the relationship you have with a contact, how you go about getting an informational interview can vary widely. In most cases, a short email that explains your situation and your interest in talking to the person is the best approach. This is certainly the case for professionals you don't know. Here is an example of an initial email you could send to a contact given to you by your CSO:

Dear Mr. Jones,

I am a student at Bowdoin College, class of 2015. I am very interested in pursuing a career in (whatever), and I was hoping I could meet with you to hear your thoughts about (the industry, company or specific job). I will be in the city the week of (whenever), however,

I could meet with you anytime that is convenient for you. My resume is attached.

Mr. Jones, I understand your time is valuable and I very much appreciate you considering this request.

Sincerely,

Ben Carpenter

You don't need to say much more. If Mr. Jones is so inclined, he can look at your resume. But most likely, he will see you because he has a loyalty to your college or because he likes to talk to, and help, young people. Business people rarely accept or reject a request for an informational interview based on how impressive a candidate appears on paper. If you don't hear from Mr. Jones within seven business days, you should follow-up with another email saying:

Dear Mr. Jones,

I just wanted to follow-up on my request for an informational interview with you. I appreciate that you are extremely busy, and if you don't have the time to meet me, I fully understand.

Mr. Jones, my trip to (wherever) is still on for the week of the (whenever), however, I could meet you anytime that is convenient for you.

Sincerely,

Ben Carpenter (Bowdoin Class of 2015)

If you still don't hear anything from Mr. Jones for 14 business days after the second email, send one more similar email. If nothing comes from the third email, I would write off Mr. Jones as a viable contact.

Special Interest Contacts

Since most people's supply of family and friends' contacts in a specific industry will be limited, your college's CSO will probably be the source of many of your contacts for informational interviews. There is, however, another potential source of contacts which are superior to those available from your CSO. I call these "special interest" contacts.

If you play a varsity sport, are in the band or choir, or are majoring in a particular area, you probably had coaches or teachers who worked with previous graduates who went into your industry of choice. Being introduced to these graduates by your special interest contact is the equivalent of a family or friends referral because you and this professional share a common interest, experience, and relationship. If your special interest coach or teacher has not been at the school a long time, then in some cases your CSO can provide the names of alumni who shared your special interest. If Mr. Jones was a referral from a special interest contact rather than the CSO, my initial email to him could have been much stronger:

> Dear Mr. Jones,
>
> I am a student at Bowdoin College, class of 2015, and I am very interested in pursuing a career in (whatever). I have played varsity lacrosse at Bowdoin for the past three years, and I asked Coach Archbell if he knew any ex-lacrosse players who worked in that industry. Coach gave me your name and suggested I contact you.
>
> Mr. Jones, I understand your time is valuable and I appreciate you considering meeting me. I will be in the city the week of (whenever), however, I could meet anytime which is convenient for you.
>
> Sincerely,
>
> Ben Carpenter
>
> P.S. Coach Archbell told me about the incredible season your team had when you were a senior—it gives our team something to shoot for this year!

These special interest contacts are not limited to contacts made in college. Any activity such as Boys and Girls Club, Boy Scouts, Girl Scouts, YMCA, church organizations, theater or music groups, or any outside of school sports teams you have been significantly involved with, have the potential to be a source of special interest contacts.

The power of special interest contacts was driven home to me during an informational interview I had with a Bowdoin College hockey player. This young man had been focused on a career in finance since before he went to college. In his senior year, however, even after four summers of finance related internships, he didn't have a job. Out of desperation, he went onto Bowdoin's alumni data base, searched former hockey alumni who now worked in finance, and picked out 12 names which seemed most promising (I was one of the 12). By the time we got together three weeks later, he had received 11 responses from these hockey alum and, after an hour phone interview, one of these alum had sent his resume to six major banks the alum's private equity firm did business with. One of these banks had already interviewed the student three times and he had just been told by the head of the leveraged finance department at that bank he would be the next hire into his group—which was the exact area of banking the Bowdoin student was most interested in! The student, as he finished telling this story, said to me with palpable awe in his voice, *"I had no idea the Bowdoin College hockey alumni network was so powerful!"*

Of course, there is a large hit or miss aspect to any specific job search outreach. Therefore, more significant than this happy story of a "hit" is the 11 prompt responses by the Bowdoin hockey alumni. *Special interest contacts will often feel a strong kinship with you and can be a very powerful source for some of your very best contacts.*

Employed Students

A fundamental business truth is companies who provide the highest quality product at the lowest price win. This is the definition of efficiency. Being efficient is *always* a good thing. If you are in college, an extremely efficient way to begin building your network is to establish relationships with fellow students who have already received a job offer from a company in your target industry. This is highly efficient because all you have to do is walk across the quad to see them!

Employed students are a fabulous place to begin your networking because they just accomplished exactly what you hope to achieve. They can give you an insider view of how they dealt with your CSO, how they built and leveraged their network, and what they believe they did well, and not so well, in their informational and job interviews.

While on-campus meetings with these employed students are likely to be less formal than meeting someone at their office, be prepared and approach them professionally. Walking up to someone between classes, fist bumping, and saying, "*Dude, congratulations on getting a job! How'd you do that?*" is not the way to go.

If you happen to know the employed student well, you should of course congratulate him in-person and ask if he would be willing to sit down sometime and talk about his job search experience. The good news is this person is likely on cloud nine, now has some free time because the pressure is off scholastically, and would love to tell you the war stories about his successful job search.

Most likely, because most colleges are reasonably large and these employed students are often in classes above you, you will not know many of them. You should treat these employed students like the professional they are about to become. Below is an example of an email to send to an employed student:

Dear Sally,

My name is Ben Carpenter and I am a sophomore (or junior) here at Bowdoin. I just heard from Mr. Smith in the Career Services Office (or from a mutual friend, or from wherever) you are going to work in advertising at BBDO—congratulations! I also am hoping to work in advertising when I graduate. Would you have time for a lunch or dinner—on or off campus, my treat. I would love to meet and hear what you learned from your job search. If that works for you, any time and place is good for me.

Sally, it must feel great to have a job lined up and the spring semester to look forward to!

Sincerely,

Ben Carpenter

After you have your meal with Sally, keep in touch and try to meet her the following year, at the BBDO offices. Hopefully, Sally will arrange for you to get informational interviews with a number of her trainee classmates, co-workers, or other industry contacts she might have. Here is an example of an email to send to Sally after she has started working at BBDO:

Dear Sally,

How are you? I am back at Bowdoin for my junior (or senior) year, and I have been thinking a great deal about our discussion over lunch six months ago. My interest in advertising has continued to increase and I would love the opportunity to come visit you at the BBDO offices whenever it is convenient for you.

As I mentioned, my primary focus is to get into the creative (or account management, or whatever) side of the business. If you have any co-workers at BBDO you think I should also talk to about the business generally, or the creative side specifically, that would be great.

Sally, the Bowdoin campus is still as beautiful as ever, but I can't wait to get to the big city!

Sincerely,

Ben Carpenter

If you are able to make contact with 10 employed students during your sophomore, junior, or senior year, who all later introduce you to two of their industry contacts or co-workers, before you know it you will have had 30 informational interviews. You will have accomplished all this after only 10 campus lunches or dinners and 10 visits to individual companies. Now that's efficient!

HOW TO GET JOB INTERVIEWS #1
ASKING FOR THE ORDER

Once you identify your target industry, your interest in getting informational interviews becomes, in part, a Trojan horse. You are only asking to speak to a person to get information about his job, company, or career, however, what you really want is to parlay your informational interview into a job interview and then a job offer! How do you do this? In sales it's called "asking for the order." At some point towards the end of an informational interview, if it hasn't come up already, you need to say, "*Your company sounds incredibly interesting and is exactly what I am interested in. Do you know of any job openings I might be able to interview for?*"

Don't feel you are imposing or being too forward by asking that question. All reasonable and experienced professionals expect you to ask that question; in fact, they may think less of you if you don't ask for the order. If the answer to your question is, "*I'm sorry but I don't know of any job openings,*" you still have two arrows left in your quiver.

- First, ask your interviewer, "*Would it be possible to get an introduction to someone in your company's HR department?*" The interviewer may know the company has a hiring freeze, however, he probably does not know an employee resigned yesterday and that there is a job opening. The people who have this information are in HR and it is always a good idea to try to speak to someone in that department. Also, even if HR says there are no jobs available now, most companies need a stable of potential hires "on deck" when, inevitably, someone leaves. So, at a minimum, your goal when speaking to HR should be to get on deck. You need to appreciate what a *huge* turnover most medium to large companies experience with junior staff. If you are able to speak to someone in HR, keep in touch with that person. You may be surprised how quickly jobs turn up.

- Second, if you feel you made some reasonable connection with the interviewer, you can, in a tactful manner, ask, "*Do you have any contacts at other companies in the industry who might be willing to speak to me?*" It takes some courage to ask that question from someone you just met, but as you already know, you can't afford to be shy.

HOW TO GET JOB INTERVIEWS #2
EMPLOYMENT WEBSITES
AND SOCIAL NETWORKING

The Internet is an important tool for young people to find job openings, but by itself it is rarely an important tool for young people to get great jobs. The reason is obvious. In today's world there are *many* more people who are qualified to do great jobs than there are great jobs. So, who gets these jobs? The answer is: The qualified people who aggressively leverage their contacts and who have the ability to sell themselves get those jobs.

Employment Websites and Identifying Job Openings

There are many employment websites with professional job listings. Two of the largest are Monster and CareerBuilder. Many smaller employment websites have a particular focus on special industries or jobs, and more of these sites are constantly being created. Use your network to help you identify the best employment websites for your specific interests. Companies often prefer to list their best jobs on these smaller, more specialized, sites since they likely will receive fewer resumes from unqualified candidates. Most of the websites are reasonably user friendly, however, once you identify a job you are interested in your work has just begun.

Social Networking and Getting Job Interviews

Prior to social networking, finding contacts to help you in your job search was a three legged stool consisting of referrals from family, friends, and your CSO. Now it is a four legged stool with the new leg being social networking. For business professionals, this space is currently dominated by LinkedIn. The value of LinkedIn is it can dramatically increase your number of contacts. *LinkedIn contacts can help you in the same ways as other contacts.* These contacts can help your resume get the attention of HR (which can lead to a job interview), provide you information about the company and the job (so you can better prepare for your interview), and in some instances these contacts can use their influence inside the company to help you become the one chosen for the job.

To use LinkedIn effectively, you need to create a high quality online profile. The LinkedIn website will give you instructions on how to create your online profile (which includes a headshot), however, like everything else, it is up to you to make it great. It is worth your time and effort to create a great LinkedIn profile, and keep it regularly updated, because this (along with your resume) is your face to the professional world. Next, you need to build a list of professionals who will accept your request for them to become what LinkedIn terms a "primary connection." Since you already know these people, your primary connections are not the real value of LinkedIn. The value of your primary connections is all the primary connections *they* have. LinkedIn calls these friends of friends "second-degree connections."

For example, if you found a job listing for your dream job at Dream Co. (and your family, friends, and CSO don't know anyone at the company), you might discover you have a LinkedIn second-degree connection at the company. You would call or email your primary connection and ask for an introduction to his primary contact at Dream Co. Continuing this scenario, your primary contact could then explain his connection to the person at Dream Co. and tell you the best way to approach this person. People think of LinkedIn as "new technology," however, it is simply another way to broaden your network. While LinkedIn has its own protocols, why and how you use your network is fundamentally the same regardless of whether your contacts come from family, friends, your CSO, or LinkedIn.

As a college student or young professional, you might have only 25 primary LinkedIn contacts. However, these 25 people could easily have over 100 primary contacts each. Voilà, now you have 2,500 new contacts who are, in essence, friends of friends. On LinkedIn you can also see third-degree connections, or friends of friends of friends. Since you don't know the same person in common, third-degree connections are generally not much more valuable than a cold call to someone in the company. You can also search LinkedIn for the names of professionals in companies where you have no connections. While you will have a lower success rate making cold calls or trying to use third- degree connections, this is still better than blindly sending in a resume and hoping to be chosen for an interview. While there is no certainty that any individual LinkedIn contact will be willing to take the time and make the effort to help you, the same goes for all contacts you solicit. Be grateful for the help you do receive and don't allow rejection to diminish your focus and determination to push forward.

HOW TO GET JOB INTERVIEWS #3
YOU NEED TO BE CREATIVE AND BOLD

You may need to be creative and bold to get some of the interviews you want most, and there are many ways to do this. Perhaps you

found a job at Technology Co. on an employment website. The
job sounds perfect for you, but you can't find any contact into
Technology Co. You know sending in a resume blindly is a waste of
time, so what can you do? How about the low tech idea of making a
large cardboard sign which reads:

Technology Co. HR

Hi! Please let me tell you why I'm the best person for the Junior
Systems Analyst job you posted on Monster.com. Thank you!

Ben

I know of people who have done versions of this tactic with fantastic results, meaning the person got an interview *and* got the job.
I know if I worked at Technology Co. I would stop and talk to the job
seeker. I would immediately remember back to my first job search
and have empathy for the young person looking for a job. I would
also admire his creativity, courage, and salesmanship.

Standing outside an office with a sign asking to speak to someone in HR may seem radical, but remember *you have nothing to
lose*. You don't have a job, you want a specific job with this specific
company, and you can't find any contact at this company. As with
interviewing in general, the worst thing that can happen to you
is you don't get the job—which is a near certainty if you don't do
something imaginative. The tougher the situation, and the less you
have to lose, the more forceful and radical your actions need to be.

A Real-Life Sweet Fairy Tale

M&M has always been the initials, and the nickname, of a friend
of mine. Her first name is Marion and her last name was Magill—
until she traded that in to become a Mussafer. Anyway, she has
children just slightly younger than mine, and a few years ago we
were discussing next steps for them, specifically how tough the job
market was. During that conversation, M&M told me the story of
her career.

She grew up in Texas and went to Univerity of Texas at Austin. She studied radio, television, and film and dreamed of moving to New York and getting a job in that business after graduation. When those four short college years ended, M&M still had the dream but no contacts in the New York media world. So, deciding to take one step at a time, she gratefully accepted the help of a friend and found a position in Manhattan as a paralegal. After a fun first year in the big city, and having "done justice" to her first job, M&M decided it was time to dust off her dream and get a job in TV production. The only problem was she *still* knew no one who worked in that industry. After sending her resume to numerous production companies and getting nowhere, she decided on a more targeted approach.

M&M did a little primary research (by watching TV) and decided NBC's *Today* show, with its wide range of hard and soft topics, was where she would most like to work. After a little non-TV watching research, she discovered the name of the executive producer of *Today* was Steve Friedman, who had been with the show for eight years and was already a legendary figure in the industry for recapturing *Today's* crown as the "King of Morning Shows."

Having experienced first-hand that sending resumes out blindly doesn't work, M&M came up with a new idea. She decided to go visit Friedman at his office—uninvited! The day after hatching this plan, M&M dressed in her best professional outfit and went to the NBC offices at Rockefeller Center. When she arrived at the huge complex she realized, much to her dismay, everyone entering had to walk through a turnstile with imposing guards standing to each side. In that split second M&M thought, "*Well, the worst thing that can happen is they throw me out,*" and with that M&M breezed through the turnstile as if she owned the place. She then got in the elevator and went up to the executive floor. When she arrived, she was pointed in the direction of Friedman's office and a few steps later she was there.

At that point, M&M got lucky because Friedman's secretary was not at her post, and he was *right there* in his office. The problem was there was also someone else in his office talking to him. Again, in a split second, M&M decided she might never get a better chance, so she walked in and said, "*Mr. Friedman, I'm sorry to interrupt you, but I wanted to give you this.*" She handed him her resume and said, "*I'll call you later this afternoon,*" and out she walked.

Later that afternoon, M&M called Friedman's office and spoke to his formerly missing-in-action secretary who, astonishingly, gave M&M a very warm, "*He's been expecting your call*" and put her through to him. Friedman said he had only a moment to talk, but asked what she was looking to do. M&M told him, and he asked her to come up with a few specific ideas for *Today* show segments and said they would have a formal phone interview next week. True to his word, the next week M&M had a phone interview with Friedman and pitched her ideas for his show. He liked a couple of them and suggested they talk further at the end of the next week.

While this seems like a fairy tale, this chapter of M&M's story does not have that kind of ending. The following week, a day before her scheduled follow-up call, Friedman left the *Today* show. In his public announcement he said he was happy to be "*walking out on top,*" which may have been great for him, but not so great for M&M.

Crushingly, it seemed she was back to square one—but not quite. M&M used the confidence she gained from her "barge-in" escapade to dig deep with more traditional networking, and she soon made a successful transition from law to production. The fairy tale reemerged over the next six years, and M&M worked her way up to the point where *she* received a job offer to become the executive producer of a production company. However, she passed on that job offer when her prince charming (that Mussafer guy) asked her to marry him, and she chose the "happily ever after" ending of becoming a wife and mother.

While M&M's story makes my cardboard sign idea look pretty tame, they both take more determination and courage to pull off than most job seekers posses. That is why they work. Not many people are willing to put themselves "out there," and professionals responsible for hiring respond well to determination and courage.

These days, precisely duplicating M&M's plan of attack would be difficult and in many cases impossible. Security has been tightened, so even entering an office building uninvited is often not possible. However, the significance of this story is not in the details; it's the creativity and guts M&M showed in vaulting over hurdles that would have kept most people firmly in their starting blocks. *If you want it bad enough, you too will find a way over the hurdles.*

HOW TO GET JOB INTERVIEWS #4 *STAYING IN TOUCH*

To get the most out of your interviews, you need to stay in touch. Specifically, you should send an email, no later than the next day, thanking the interviewer for his time. You also need to periodically touch base with all your contacts throughout your job search.

Thank You Emails for Informational Interviews

Thank you notes for an informational interview should reference one specific thing the interviewer said and also reference your point of contact with him. While handwritten notes have a nice old-fashioned feel, for most business correspondence, including thank you notes, *I prefer email because it is instantaneous, easy to open, easy to refer back to, and easy for the recipient to respond to if he so chooses.* The following is an example of a follow-up email to send after an informational interview:

> Dear Mr. Jones,
>
> Thank you for taking the time to meet with me today. I really enjoyed our conversation and the point you made about (whatever) was of great interest to me. The next time I see Mr. Johnson, I will be sure to thank him for putting me in contact with you.
>
> Also, thank you for introducing me to Mr. Henry in your Human Resources Department and giving me the name of your friend, Ms. Heller. Her company sounds very interesting, and I will try to contact her tomorrow.
>
> Mr. Jones, I very much appreciate all your help.
>
> Sincerely,
>
> Ben Carpenter

Now *that* is how you write a thank you email. After you meet Ms. Heller be sure to send another, very brief, email to Mr. Jones thanking him again.

Thank You Emails for Job Interviews

A thank you note for a job interview is really just a continuation of the interview. It is another opportunity for you to show why you are a great candidate (hopefully the best candidate) for the job. The following is an example of such a note:

> Dear Ms. Murphy,
>
> I want you to know how much I enjoyed my interview with you today. From our conversation, and my earlier conversations with Jim Campbell and Susan Wilson in your sales department, I can't tell you how excited I am about the possibility of working for your company.
>
> Ms. Murphy, I am certain you have many great candidates for this junior sales position. I promise, however, no one will work harder, no

one will be a better team player, and no one wants this job more than I do.

If there is any additional information I can provide as you are going through your hiring process, I am always available.

Sincerely,

Ben Carpenter

Call Logs and Shaking Trees

Unless you have a photographic memory, you need to keep a call log after all information and job interviews which briefly reviews who you spoke to and any significant things that were said. Many businesses require their salespeople write call reports after all client meetings and, since getting a job *is* your job, you should do this too. (A related step is to be certain that you put any specific follow-up actions into your calendar.)

Also, unless you have a very short job search, you need to periodically reconnect with all your contacts. I call this "shaking trees." If you have ever been apple picking, you know the easiest and quickest way to get your hands on the best out of reach apples is to shake the trees. This is what follow-up emails can do for you. Although some of your follow-up emails will not be individually crafted, you should individually write emails for your most promising contacts. Your call log will help remind you what topics to refer to for these individually crafted emails.

You should reconnect with HR professionals every month. It is part of the job of HR personnel to keep in touch with potential hires, so frequent contact is appropriate. For informational interview contacts, you should touch base every three months. These non-HR professions have day jobs unrelated to your job search and you don't want to become a pest by too frequent contact. Below is an example of a basic follow-up email to an informational interview contact which could easily be edited to become a more individually crafted note:

Dear Mr. Jones,

My job search has continued to progress well. I haven't yet achieved my goal of getting a job in (whatever) industry, but I know I am making good headway. From speaking to people like you, my determination to get a job in this industry has grown as my understanding of the business has grown.

Mr. Jones, thank you again for all your help and advice. If you can think of anyone else in your company, or the industry, I should speak to, I would greatly appreciate it.

Sincerely,

Ben Carpenter

WHAT TO SAY DURING INTERVIEWS #1
IT'S NOT ABOUT YOU

Probably the single biggest misunderstanding that people, young and old, have about interviewing concerns the message they need to get across to the interviewer. They think their goal should be to impress the interviewer with how smart, accomplished, and nice they are. Wrong! Think about it this way: does a professional baseball coach care whether a player is smart and nice, or whether that player can help the team win? *The interview, first and foremost, is about convincing the interviewer you are the best person available to help his company become more successful.*

Especially during job interviews, this insight should inform every word that comes out of your mouth. The interview is not about solving *your* problem (getting a job). Rather, the interview is all about you helping the interviewer solve *his* problem, which is finding the best person to help his company succeed (by the way, that's you!).

Before Avery interviewed for her job at the TV show, we discussed this "it's not about you" issue at length and she came up with a plan. At the end of her interview, as she was shaking hands with the co-executive producer, Avery said, "*It has been great meeting you and if you give me a chance, I know I can help make this new show a success.*"

Saying something so bold is akin to handling nitroglycerin: if not done carefully, it can blow up in your face. The negative is you can come across as arrogant. The positive is you can come across as confident and, most importantly, focused on helping the company succeed.

WHAT TO SAY DURING INTERVIEWS #2
INFORMATIONAL AND JOB INTERVIEWS ARE DIFFERENT

Since informational and job interviews are similar but distinct, the question is: do you say different things in the two types of interviews? The answer is both yes and no. One major difference for an informational interview is you will be asking more general questions about the job, company, or industry. Also, during informational interviews it is generally a good idea to ask the interviewer about his job and career. In a job interview, the interviewer will expect you already know a good deal about the job you are interviewing for, and he certainly does not expect you to ask much, if anything, about his job and career.

Going back to my interview with the Morgan Guy, I knew it was a job interview, but I didn't know what I was doing and treated it like an informational interview. Needless to say, the Morgan Guy wasn't confused about what he was doing, and he correctly wrote me off as an unprepared rookie who was not ready for the big leagues.

So, how are informational interviews and job interviews the same? For both informational and job interviews you want the interviewer to feel his company would be better off if you worked there. Much of the advice in these 10 "*WHAT TO SAY DURING INTERVIEWS*" sections is applicable to both informational and job interviews. The only difference is for most informational interviews a softer sell is appropriate, while a harder sell is generally more appropriate for job interviews. This difference can be quite subtle, as subtle as saying the same words in a gentler (for informational interviews) or more aggressive (for job interviews) tone of voice. Sometimes, it is not entirely clear whether you are being granted an informational interview or having a job interview. In those cases, always assume it's a job interview.

For both informational and job interviews, the way you answer questions is as important as what you say. First, listen carefully, and if you didn't fully understand the question, ask for clarification. Also, it sometimes makes sense to pause and think about the question for a moment before plunging headlong into an answer. Finally, always say, "*I don't know*" if that's the honest answer. Intelligent and confident people tend to say, "*I don't know*" much more often than less intelligent and less confident people.

WHAT TO SAY DURING INTERVIEWS #3
HOW TO PREPARE

Since an interviewer does not generally know you, he will assume the way you prepare for your interview is indicative of how you will do a job. You, of course, want the interviewer to believe you are intelligent, diligent, and if given the opportunity will do everything in your power to do a great job. The way you communicate this to the interviewer is by being fully prepared for the interview. Here are a few tricks to impress interviewers that you know how to prepare.

Online Research

First, study the company's website, paying particular attention to the "about" and "press" sections and work this information into your interviews. One example of how to use this information is to say: "*I saw on your website you just opened a new office in London. Do you see Europe as a big growth area for your company? Do you think the European sovereign debt crisis will be an opportunity or challenge for you?*" Additionally, before all interviews research the person you are meeting, using Google and LinkedIn, to discover any personal or professional information about the interviewer you might be able to use.

Get Informational Interviews at a Company Before Your Job Interview

The most important advice I can give you about how to get a great job is to arrange for informational interviews with junior staff at a company before you have a job interview. Arrange these informational interviews by using your entire network: family, friends, your CSO, and LinkedIn. These pre-job informational interviews are hugely valuable to get you up to speed on a company and the requirements of the job you are interviewing for. An example of how to impress an interviewer is to say, "*I was just talking to your salesman, George Jones, whom I went to college with and he said your new product launch was going terrifically well! How big do you think this product can be for you?*" Having already spoken to employees of the company will allow you to:

- Display your initiative and ability to network.
- Have an intelligent conversation about the company or industry and ask intelligent questions.
- Highlight how seriously you are taking your job search and how seriously you are taking your interview with the employee responsible for hiring.

- Differentiate you from your competitors because few college students or young professionals appreciate the importance of the pre-job informational interviews.

The Power of Primary Research

Do primary research on companies before you interview. An example would be if you were interviewing for a job as a junior account manager at an advertising firm, Ad Co., whose biggest client is Brand X cars. Prior to your interview, consider visiting the local Brand X dealership and talk to the manager about his business and the challenges he has selling cars. Later, in your Ad Co. job interview, mention your visit to the dealership and the dealership manager's issues. This conversation is certain to impress your interviewer and will *dramatically* set you apart from other candidates.

WHAT TO SAY DURING INTERVIEWS #4 *HOW TO SELL YOURSELF—PUNCHY VIGNETTES*

There is a very old and very true saying that, "The world belongs to salesmen." It doesn't matter how outstanding your product (or personal expertise) is, if you can't sell people on its high quality it is like the tree falling in the forest—no one will hear it and no one will care. Therefore, as in any form of advertising, you need to think hard about the best way to sell the product. Since you are the product for sale, your job is to convince the interviewer you are the best person to help his company succeed. But how do you do that?

- First, think through what you believe to be your greatest strengths: intelligence, determination, creativity, writing, or whatever else you do well.

- Second, think about how these skills can be matched to the job you are seeking.

- Third, compose brief but punchy vignettes (which generally should not be longer than a minute) about how your strengths can help you do the job. You may have an opportunity to use your punchy vignettes as answers to questions asked of you, or you may need to bring them up yourself during the interview. Either way, after enough practice these vignettes are certain to help you sell yourself since they compellingly and succinctly communicate to your interviewer why he needs to hire you. Also, job seekers often leave interviews regretting what they said—or forgot to say. Having punchy vignettes at the ready will greatly reduce the number of interview regrets you experience.

For College Students

If you are a college student interviewing for your first job as a customer service (or sales) representative, an example of a punchy vignette could be:

> I feel I learned a great deal about customer service (or sales) from working as a waiter at a very busy restaurant for the past two summers. The owner is a pretty tough guy and he doesn't kowtow to anyone. However, when a customer made unreasonable demands he couldn't, or wouldn't, accommodate, he always patiently and respectfully explained why. I saw this guy regularly tame the craziest customers and by the time he was done telling them no, they were thanking him! I learned an awful lot about customer service (or sales) from the owner and by the end of the summer I felt I could manage my customers almost as well as he could.

For Young Professionals

If you've already been working but are now looking to switch jobs, companies, or even careers, be certain to highlight how your previous job experience can be relevant and helpful in the position you are seeking. If the new job is very similar to your old job, the task of coming up with punchy vignettes should be easy. However, let's look at a tougher situation. Imagine you want to make a radical career change from an elementary school teacher to corporate human resources professional. Here is an example of a punchy vignette you could use during your interview:

> It might seem a stretch to equate the skills it takes to be a fifth grade teacher to a job in human resources. However, after a number of informational interviews with HR professionals, I can see how some of my experiences as a teacher do translate. It is important to every parent that I make their child's issues my number one priority, but this is impossible to do when there are 15 to 20 students in my class. However, I've become quite good at listening to parents, watching their children, and coming up with unique ways to manage my time. It is all about treating each child as an individual. I quickly learn what personal attention each student needs, scholastically or socially, and schedule my time around all my students' needs. I have been told having all employees feel their concerns are my number one priority is a valuable skill I could bring to a job in HR. However, I also know there is a great deal I don't know about HR and I very much look forward to learning.

Be Excited

Most people are scared when they interview and because of this don't show excitement about the job they are seeking. It is almost impossible to get an interviewer excited about hiring you if you don't exude and express genuine excitement about the industry, company, and job.

If you had any internships in the industry, talking about that experience is a perfect vehicle to show your enthusiasm. For instance, if you are interviewing for a job in public relations, your punchy vignette could be:

My internship last summer at P.R. Co. was fantastic. I had the opportunity to work on two very interesting projects for A Co. and B Co. Both of these companies were dealing with serious crises relating to product defects. I enjoyed digging into the problems to understand them in depth and help brainstorm the best ways for these companies to use public relations to speak to their employees, customers, and shareholders. In the case of B Co., I wrote two of the press releases addressing the situation. Unfortunately, P.R. Co. currently has a hiring freeze, however, I got along extremely well with my boss and she volunteered to speak to anyone concerning my performance. While I learned a good deal of specifics last summer about public relations, most importantly, I learned I love the business!

If I'm responsible for filling that junior public relations position, I would feel you just hit it out of the park, and I would want you on my team! Likewise, it is very effective to show genuine excitement about the possibility of working at the specific company you are interviewing for. For instance, during a job interview you might say:

I think it would be great if I could get a job with Awesome Co. The employees I've talked to seem to really love the company and the way you guys do (whatever) is very exciting. The chance to work in a (small start-up, a major international firm, an industry leader, or whatever) seems like a perfect place for me to learn the business and help this great company continue to win.

The ultimate achievement is to get your interviewer *more* excited about the company he *already* works for. This may sound implausible, however, I've had numerous interviewees do exactly that to me (*and I wanted to hire all of them!*).

Open Up About Who You Are and What Motivates You

Opening up about yourself and what motivates you may not fit the tone or flow of every interview. However, if you can be honest, and show the appropriate amount of emotion, it could easily be the strongest part of your sales pitch. For instance, if I were a college student or young professional interviewing for a job I could say:

> If I am lucky enough to get this job I will be absolutely determined to succeed. I love my father and he taught me many life lessons, including how to never give up, but for a variety of reasons he never had the professional success he hoped for. That has been a source of financial hardship for my family and emotional anguish for him. I will do anything and everything possible to be a highly valued employee of this company because I can not allow what happened to my father to happen to me.

Conversely, depending on your life experience, you might say:

> My motivation to succeed comes from watching my father and seeing the satisfaction and happiness he has enjoyed in his career. My father is a (policeman, teacher, doctor, lawyer, businessman, salesman, or whatever) and he is great at his job. He loves to go to work every day and I know he goes above and beyond what the job requires to be the best. He is also a great father and husband and I am absolutely determined to follow the example he has set. I can't wait to start my career and put to work the lessons I learned from him.

Every interviewer wants to know what motivates a job candidate. Most interviewers will appreciate not having to guess. *If done well, opening up about who you are can also create an emotional connection to the interviewer which could prove to be the difference in you getting the job rather than some other equally, or perhaps even more, qualified candidate.*

WHAT TO SAY DURING INTERVIEWS #5
TALKING TO YOUR RESUME

At most interviews, especially job interviews, the interviewer will ask you questions concerning your resume. You never know what will catch the eye of an interviewer, so you need to have an idea about how to frame everything on your resume in the best possible light. Not all your answers will qualify as punchy vignettes, but all your answers need to help the interviewer understand why he needs to hire you. For instance, for a job in public relations, advertising, or marketing you could be asked, "*Did you enjoy being an English major?*" While your answer could be lengthy, an effective brief answer would be, "*I enjoyed it a great deal and one of the reasons I am so excited about public relations is the opportunity to put my strong writing skills to use.*"

Another example, for a job in sales, would be an answer to the question, "*Did you like being in a fraternity?*" I believe lengthy conversations about fraternity life are a bad idea for most interviews, but a good answer would be, "*I enjoyed my fraternity a great deal, but what I liked the most was giving my sales pitch to freshmen why my fraternity was the best. I have always enjoyed the challenge of getting people to see things the way I do, and that is what excites me about sales.*"

Also you should be prepared to address any potential negatives in your resume. The best way to deal with such questions is to be disarmingly forthright about the issue and what you learned or how you handled a situation. For instance:

Interviewer: So, why did it take you six years to graduate from college?

You: My first year at college I went crazy with all the freedom. I had a great time, but I also realized I wasn't focused on anything except the parties. I decided to take a year off to (backpack around the world, work in a restaurant, work for a non-profit, or whatever). I enjoyed the experience and decided to do it for a second year. When I did get back to school, I had grown up enough to know where I wanted to go and what I needed to do scholastically to help me get there. That is why I majored in (whatever) and also why I am here talking to you today.

Or perhaps you are a college graduate who hated your first job and are interviewing for your next job:

Interviewer: So, why were you at First Co. only six months?

You: First Co. was a terrific experience for me. I loved my co-workers and boss and I believe the product (or service) is outstanding. My job was to be in the office and cold call prospects. I did a good job, but I quickly realized having no face-to-face contact with the customers wasn't satisfying to me. I know I would excel in a sales (or service) position that has a good deal of direct customer contact, and that is one of the reasons I am so excited about this job opportunity!

In both cases, the hypothetical you was able to take a potential negative on your resume and turn it around to a positive while sounding (and being) very honest. These are the kinds of answers to tough questions interviewers respond well to.

Finally, questions about any sport, band, choir, or other organizations you participated in which have a team element are a perfect lead-in for you to affirm your love for some combination of teamwork, leadership, and winning. Although such statements can sound trite or phony, they won't if you believe them and have practiced them.

WHAT TO SAY DURING INTERVIEWS #6
HOW TO BE GENERAL AND SPECIFIC

When you are having an informational or a job interview with a large company, you may be asked, "*What specific area of this company (or industry) do you want to work in?*" If you give the response I have heard countless times, "*I don't know…I would take any job available*" you will appear desperate, unfocused, and unprepared. Conversely, you shouldn't say, "*I want to work in (a specific) department*" because that department may not have any jobs available. This is a difficult tightrope to walk. An example of a good balance to strike would be to say:

> I had the chance to talk to Sue Smith in your (whatever) area and I also had numerous informational interviews with other professionals in this industry. I believe (insert your specific job interest) would be a great fit for my (specific talents and background). That said, I realize there is still a great deal I don't know about this (company or industry) and my first goal is to get a job, learn the business, and help my company succeed in any way I can.

If I were the interviewer, I'd be impressed. You just showed me you did your homework, thought logically about matching your interests, talents, and background with your career, and are practical, flexible, and would be focused on helping my company succeed. Pretty darn good for just three sentences!

WHAT TO SAY DURING INTERVIEWS #7 *UNDERSTANDING THE GAME AROUND YOU*

Every day in the world generally, and the world of business specifically, people do seemingly brilliant, stupid, admirable, and despicable things and it is great fun to keep up with it all. The best way to get all the information you need is to subscribe to the online or print versions of the *New York Times, Wall Street Journal,* or other specific trade publications. It will be nearly impossible for you to survive and thrive in the big leagues if you don't know what is going on in the game around you.

I am always impressed by college students who display an understanding of relevant current events. For instance, I was impressed when a college student said during an interview, "*I saw in today's Wall Street Journal that pension funds were increasing their purchases of corporate and mortgage bonds. I assume this must be good news for your company.*"

WHAT TO SAY DURING INTERVIEWS #8
WHAT NOT TO SAY

In most informational interviews, and in all initial job interviews, don't ask about salary, benefits, working conditions and hours, promotion opportunities, or any negative issues concerning the company. If you get further along, hopefully after receiving a job offer, you can ask those questions.

One of my favorite questions as an interviewer is to ask, "*What are you going to do if you aren't able to get a job in finance?*" I always get interesting responses such as, "*My father owns a furniture store and I would go work there.*" However, there is only one right answer to that question and it is, "*I haven't thought about that at all. I am totally focused on getting a job in this industry and I am absolutely confident I will accomplish this goal. I would love to work for your company, but if that doesn't happen I know I will get a job somewhere because I am not going to stop trying.*"

Finally, if you are looking to switch jobs, you will often be asked what you didn't like about your previous job. Look out for that one—it's also a trap. *In a job interview you should never be negative about anything.* While interviewing, you should always say your previous job, boss, or career was good, but you are even more excited about this new opportunity. In sales, the letters ABC stand for "Always Be Closing." In interviews, since you are selling yourself, you need to ABC and to do that you need to ABP—"Always Be Positive."

WHAT TO SAY DURING INTERVIEWS #9
QUESTIONS TO ASK

Asking intelligent questions is an important part of interviewing. This is not intended to be a list of the best questions to ask because the best questions are specific to the industry, company, job, interviewer, and interviewee. However, these questions will give you an idea about the types of questions you should ask during informational interviews and how these differ from questions for job interviews. Since I spent most of my career in sales and because most companies have a sales department, I have chosen questions for that occupation. However, you can substitute most job descriptions and ask similar questions. Some of these questions are the practical application of the principles covered in the previous sections. *For informational interviews, you should be prepared to ask most of the questions. For most job interviews, it's likely the interviewer will ask most of the questions. However, the quality of the questions you do ask during a job interview is extremely important.*

Informational Interview Questions

1. What do you like about sales?

2. What do you like about this industry (or company)?

3. Is it typical for people in this company to start in sales or do you need work in other areas first?

4. Have you worked at other companies? Was selling much different there?

5. What does it take to be a great salesperson?

6. What should I know about this job or industry we haven't discussed?

7. If you were a college senior again, knowing what you now know, how would you go about trying to get a job in this industry?

8. Asking for the Order #1: Do you know if there are any jobs in this company which would make sense for me to interview for? (If the answer is "no" then move on to questions 9 and 10).

9. Asking for the Order #2: Would you be willing to introduce me to someone in Human Resources?

10. Asking for the Order #3: Talking to you about selling in this industry has gotten me even more excited about it as a career.

Do you know people at other firms you would feel comfortable introducing me to?

Job Interview Questions

1. I had the opportunity to talk to two members of your sales team and they seem very excited about the new product launch next month. Do you expect to be hiring more salespeople as part of that initiative?

2. From talking to a few of your competitors, it seems they are quite envious of your sales penetration into China. How did you guys accomplish that?

3. I Googled the top clients of your company and I found one where my college's CSO had a senior contact. I spoke to this person about your company and he was very complimentary. He particularly liked the unique way you coordinated sales and product support. Do you see this as a competitive advantage for your company?

4. I want you to know I am willing to relocate anywhere in the world. Are there any regions that are specifically looking to increase their sales staff?

5. If I were lucky enough to get this sales job my goal would be to become the #1 salesperson you have. I would love to hear what you think it takes to be a great salesperson in this industry and company.

WHAT TO SAY DURING INTERVIEWS #10 *QUESTIONS YOU MAY BE ASKED*

It is impossible to anticipate what questions you may be asked during an informational or job interview. However, in addition to being prepared to talk about your resume (and especially about any previous job experience you may have on your resume), there are other questions you should be prepared for. Following is a list of 10 of the most frequently asked interview questions:

1. Tell me about yourself.

2. What are your strengths?

3. What are your weaknesses?

4. What are your goals?

5. Why do you want to work in this industry?

6. Why do you want to work at this company?

7. Why do you think you would do well at this job?

8. Tell me about your job search. Who have you talked to?

9. What's the last book you read?

10. What do you like to do for fun?

Keep in mind that an interview is not a test to see if you can come up with the right answers. Rather, it is your opportunity to sell yourself as the best person to help the company succeed. While what you say is important, even more important is that you come across as honest, confident, enthusiastic, determined, and prepared. It may sound like interviewers are asking for an awful lot, however, employers with great jobs to offer will *not* hire you if they think you will be only an average or even a good employee. *Good is not good enough! You only get hired for a great job if you are able to inspire the interviewer that you will be an outstanding employee.* Keep this in mind as you compose your punchy vignettes and think about how you will answer these most likely asked questions.

BE MORE AGGRESSIVE

As you read the sample emails, punchy vignettes, and questions to ask, I would not be surprised if, because of their overtly aggressive tone, you once again said to yourself, "*You've got to be kidding!*" Despite evidence to the contrary, I do not believe everyone should aspire to be NFL linebacker, foam-at-the-mouth aggressive. You need to be who you are and there are many people who are hugely successful without being hugely aggressive. However, because business is so competitive, I believe most people need to push themselves to be more aggressive.

For instance, on a hypothetical 1 to 10 scale of socially acceptable aggressiveness, if you are naturally a 3 to 4, you should push yourself to be a 5 to 6. If you are a 7 to 8, push yourself to be a 9 to 10. If you are the rare person who is already a 10, make sure you don't cross the line and become a 12 to 13. You don't want people ducking for cover every time you walk into a room.

Displaying aggressiveness during the interview process is especially challenging for college students and young professionals because you are still learning the game. However, it is even more important for you to display aggressiveness than experienced professionals. Why? Because college students and young professionals have less developed skills and track records to impress interviewers. When interviewers are evaluating young people, they are looking for individuals who have *potential* to do a great job. *Displaying your aggressiveness in an interview is an important way to convince a recruiter you have what it takes to be great.*

As in the example of standing outside a company's office with a sign asking to speak to someone in HR, being aggressive in interviews means being willing to take some chances. Unless you have an inside track to get a specific job, you should be willing to be aggressive and take some chances with how assertive you are. *Finally, much of what could be described as aggression is actually honesty. You need to believe you will work hard, be a great teammate, and do an outstanding job. Most interviewers will be impressed you don't beat around the bush and have the intelligence and courage to directly address the only question they really care about: "Are you the person I should hire—and why?"*

READ YOUR INTERVIEWER

Job interviews can vary in length, but most common is 30 minutes, and a typical interview is:

- First, for one to five minutes, establish an easy rapport with the interviewer. For informational interviews this mostly happens while discussing your common connection (college, family, friends, and so on). For job interviews it could be the weather, your travels to the interview, a recent major sporting event, or any light topic.

- Second, for 20 to 28 minutes, discuss substantive matters related to your interest in the industry, company, and job. This conversation allows you to highlight your intelligence, preparation, and ability to help the company by periodically using your punchy vignettes. Also, this is when you will be asked to talk about your resume.

- Third, for one to five minutes, toward the end of your interview, look for the opportunity to emphasize your determination and aggressiveness. You should have also shown these traits earlier in the interview, but it is important to revisit this theme since the last words you speak are the first ones an interviewer remembers. Since you will be competing against other candidates who have pleasant personalities and good resumes, this final push can get you over the top to become the one who gets the great job.

Of course, the interviewer is in charge and he can direct the topics and tone of the interview as he sees fit. One of the most important interviewing skills is to be able to read your interviewer to understand what he is looking for in a job candidate. This skill comes from paying attention and practice. In this way, you are like a fly fisherman. As you practice and get better at fly fishing, you learn which flies, presented in which ways, are the most likely to catch fish. Every stream and every day are different, however, and what worked great yesterday might not today. This is why experienced fly fishermen change flies, and change the way they present and cast the flies, until they find out what gets the fish to bite *that* day.

With practice, you will learn what content and presentation generally seem to work the best as well as have the ability to modify both as you read your interviewer's reactions. You should not be a total chameleon, but you know you are a somewhat different person when you are around your close friends, parents, grandparents, coaches, and so on. Adjusting your personality to each interviewer is no different. For instance, if your interviewer has the personality of a football coach, you will likely be well served to emphasize your aggressiveness. If your interviewer has the personality of a librarian, emphasize your thoughtfulness. While still being you, use your judgment, perception, and intelligence to adapt what you say, and how you say it, to get the interviewer on the hook and ultimately land the job.

Finally, it is probably a very good thing for your personal development to have practice adapting and being responsive to others. The old expression "absolute power corrupts absolutely" is applicable not only to despots. It is not unusual for any person in a position of power to, over time, lose the ability (or perhaps simply the desire) to adapt to others. This is because often everyone around a powerful person (salesmen, hangers-on, and the like) are anxious to adapt and please that person. Sadly, the result can be a severely limited and ossified personality. *So don't resent or fear having to adapt to other people; look at it as exercise to make your own personality stronger and more limber.*

ALL ABOUT INTERNSHIPS

Back in the Dark Ages, when I was in high school and college, no one (at least that I knew) had professional summer internships. I cut grass for a landscaper, screwed together storm windows in a factory, worked at restaurants, worked on a farm, and attended the U.S. Marine Corps Officers Candidate School in Quantico, Virginia. I'm not sure if today's proliferation of professional internships are good for a young person's development; there is something to be said for experiencing manual labor or having a Marine drill sergeant yell at you for 16 hours a day. However, professional internships are now a fact of life for young people looking for a leg up in getting a great full-time job out of college. These internships are important in order to:

- Allow you to explore a particular job or industry.
- Develop the skills necessary for the working world.
- Bolster your resume by showing initiative, determination, and focus in obtaining a professional summer internship.
- Broaden your network of contacts.
- Sharpen your professional conversational skills for your full-time job search.

Internships have become so important to achieving your goal of getting a great full-time job that you need to be flexible and imaginative in seeking them out. Some colleges have long winter or holiday vacations, and students can get internships during these breaks they might not be able to get during summers. Another way to "skin the cat" is to take a semester off to do an internship, or combine an internship with a study abroad program. Also, after college graduation, if you have not been fortunate enough to get a full-time job, internships can be a great way to go. In fact, some companies are now reluctant to hire any young person full-time until they have proved themselves through an internship at their company.

My advice on internships is identical to getting a full-time job—start early! Today, many of the most competitive full-time jobs are already taken by September of senior year. Why? Because the jobs are grabbed by students who had internships at these companies after junior year. This is particularly prevalent in finance and consulting. While many of you will not be interested in finance or consulting, starting early is still critically important for all students looking to get great internships and, ultimately, great full-time jobs in any industry. *Starting early means trying to get a professional internship after your sophomore, or even freshman, year in college.* The competition keeps getting tougher and better prepared, so you need to respond in kind. If you are a senior, or graduate, without any professional internships on your resume—don't despair. Like most other challenges, this can be overcome with focus, hard work, and determination.

Junior and Senior Years of High School

For the junior and senior years of high school, summer professional internships are not important from a resume-building perspective. My personal bias is that these summers are a good time for young adults to experience the non-professional working world. Jobs in restaurants, factories, retail stores, and so on are valuable experiences which instill good work habits, engender an understanding and empathy for others, and hopefully lead to an appreciation for the challenges, opportunities, and rewards of a professional career. However, this is a reasonable time to begin thinking generally about what career path might interest you because that could help you determine where to attend college and what you choose to study.

Freshman Year of College

A professional summer internship is not necessary after your freshman year of college. Employers do not expect to see relevant work experience from your freshman year summer, partly because so few professional internships are available. However, if you happen to have a strong contact (most likely a parent or a friend's parent) who can get you a summer internship—great! The biggest benefit of a post-freshman year professional internship is to help you determine if an industry interests you.

What is important freshman year is to try to line up your post-sophomore year internship. It may sound ridiculous to focus on internships a full year forward, but it is critically important because sophomore year internships are in short supply. If you have a personal contact who has a sophomore internship available, *you* need to be the first one to ask for it. If you wait until sophomore year to ask you run a strong risk of having someone else grab that precious opportunity before you get your act together.

Sophomore Year of College

During your sophomore year, a professional internship starts to matter for building your resume because you are only one step away from interviewing for the all-important post-junior year internships. You need to use your entire network to decide what internship you want and how to get it. While a few large companies offer an "open" application process, there are frequently only a small number of positions available, and many of those are taken by candidates with strong personal contacts inside that company. So, you must fight fire with fire. You need to work all the contacts you can muster, and interview for as many internships as possible, to increase your chances of obtaining a professional internship in your industry of choice.

Junior Year of College

The internship most important for many students is the one after their junior year. Increasingly, companies across a wide range of industries offer a substantial percentage of their full-time post-graduation jobs to interns who worked for them the previous summer. Happily, junior internships are much more plentiful than freshman or sophomore internships and the application process is a more level playing field. It is likely your CSO will be able to help you ferret out junior year internship opportunities and, of course, you should tap any and all of your personal contacts.

For companies set up to offer junior year interns jobs after graduation, the percentage of interns offered a full-time post-graduation job is often in the 50 to 70% range. If you are talented and fortunate enough to get your dream junior year internship—go crazy! By crazy I mean you want to be the *best* intern *ever* at that company. Possibly no two months of your entire working career will be more important. Dress appropriately *every* day, try to establish great relationships with everyone you meet, get to work earlier, work harder than everyone else, be creative, be a good teammate, and network constantly. Once you get back to school with a job offer in hand, there will be *lots* of time to goof off, but during your internship you need to be "all business!"

The advice in the next Chapter, "How to Do a Great Job," is as applicable to interns as it is to full-time employees. One piece of advice you will hear from my executive assistant, Lori, "*First impressions are everything*" is especially true for interns. Most internships are 10 weeks or less, so the first impression you make is likely to also be the last impression you leave behind. Remember, it is important that *everyone* you come into contact with, including other interns, feel positively about you. While other interns are competing with you for job offers, you need to treat them *all* with consideration and respect. It is likely the intern coordinator will know how interns feel about each other, and if you are held in high regard by your peers, you will likely be held in high regard by the intern coordinator, who often has an important vote in the decision about who receives job offers.

If you aren't fully engaged each day, it is your responsibility to come up with ideas on how you can do more. Sometimes it will be appropriate for you to come up with an idea and just do it, and sometimes you will need to clear it with your boss. However, you can't wait to be told what to do. You need to be proactive and creative. (One of the best sources of ideas for how you can be productive is to ask junior employees at the company who were recently interns themselves.)

Finally, it is important to note that even if your company does not generally offer interns post-graduation jobs, there are always exceptions. Also, even if you don't get a job offer, you may want to ask your internship boss, or internship coordinator, for a recommendation. *Always remember, your first priority is to do a great job during your junior year internship.*

Post-Graduation

Despite my exhortation to focus on getting a great junior year internship (leading to a post-graduation job offer), only a very small percentage of students will accomplish that goal. Perhaps you didn't know what you want to do, you didn't get an internship, or the company you interned with was not set up to offer interns full-time jobs. Whatever the reason, if you end up post-graduation without a job you will have a *lot* of company. Most of your classmates will be in the same boat. Post-graduation, you may be able to quickly get a great full-time job by following the advice in *The Bigs*. However, it may make sense to do a post- graduation internship to get an understanding of an industry, or to get your foot in the door of a particular company.

HOW TO USE HEADHUNTERS

We are not talking about savages who cut off and save the heads of enemies as trophies. Nor are we talking about athletes who intentionally seek to injure an opponent. Rather, we are talking about the slightly less thrilling, yet nevertheless important, group of people who make their living by helping match professionals with appropriate jobs.

Despite recruiting and hiring many people during my career, I have had little professional experience with headhunters. Most of my career was at Greenwich Capital and we were in the unusual position of having the best and the brightest in our industry knocking on our door.

Happily, my ignorance will not be a handicap for *The Bigs* because my good friend, Larry Ross, is a headhunter. Twenty years ago, Larry founded Ross & Company that specializes in placing executives into health care companies owned by private equity firms. Larry is a big guy, who was a class ahead of me at Hotchkiss, and he went on to play football at Yale. Being a headhunter is a perfect job for Larry because he has a warm and embracing personality, a quick wit, and is a keen observer of the human condition. Finally, Larry is a member of my favorite golf course, Fishers Island, so it's a good idea for me to say nice things about him. But I digress. Here is what Larry had to say about headhunters and how they can help you maximize your career opportunities:

> Hi! I'm Larry Ross and I've been a headhunter, also known as an executive recruiter, for almost 30 years. Before I get into the nitty-gritty of the business, I think it is important for you to understand that headhunters are wonderful human beings whose only interest is making the world a better place. Just kidding…headhunters, like everyone else, do what we do to make a living. However, the service we provide can be an important tool to help you achieve your goals. Not surprisingly, the goals of the young people I speak to today aren't much different than mine and my friends' all those years ago. Most

everyone wants an interesting, challenging, and lucrative job and career. If this is you, I have one overarching piece of advice: Do a great job at your job. I know that sounds ludicrously obvious, but any career plans that aren't built on the foundation of your previous outstanding job performance are built on sand. There are numerous strategies that can help you get noticed by headhunters, so you are positioned to be contacted about the most exciting jobs in your chosen field. However, understand that if you follow my first piece of advice, and do a great job, headhunters will find you. That is what we do: search for, identify, and then recruit the best talent to come work for our clients.

Headhunters rarely pursue recent college graduates because companies are not willing to pay headhunters to find candidates for entry level jobs. Even if companies were willing to hire headhunters to fill junior roles, there would not be enough money to be made by the recruiter. Headhunters, however, make outstanding informational interview contacts. I recommend you use all your personal and college contacts to try to find a headhunter who will give you career advice. As headhunters, we are professionals in the career planning business and if you can get to one of us during college, or early in your career, you will be ahead of the game.

The vast majority of jobs headhunters fill are assignments given to us by a company. In other words, it's not like when you hire a lawyer and then he represents you. Instead, a company hires a headhunter to fill a job, and the headhunter goes out and tries to find the best person for that job. The headhunter works for the company—not for you. So the question is: how to increase the odds headhunters will find you and "sell" you as the best person for the great job they are charged with filling. The first step is to, as early as possible in your career, get on the radar of the 8 to 10 headhunting firms who specialize in your industry. Regardless of your industry, these will include the five majors:

1. Korn Ferry International
2. Heidrick & Struggles
3. Spencer Stuart
4. Russell Reynold Associates
5. Egon Zehnder International

After these five global firms, that operate across most industries, each specific industry will have a number of smaller firms that specialize in one or two industries such as financial services, consulting, media, health care, advertising, and so on. or. As with any job search, you cannot expect to send your resume to headhunting firms and get their attention. You need to network, find out which partner at each headhunting firm is most focused on your segment of your industry, and send a cover letter and resume to that person, remembering to highlight any personal contact you might have in common. After that, you should update your resume every few years and resend it to these 8 to 10 headhunting firms. Also, never pass up a chance to network (e.g., at industry conferences) with headhunters involved in your industry.

Depending on which industry you enter, or the happenstance of your career progression, headhunters may end up being a critical or nonexistent factor for you. Different industries utilize headhunters to different degrees. However, in most industries, virtually all senior professional by the end of their careers will have considered an opportunity via a headhunter driven search, and at least 30% will have obtained one or more of their jobs through a headhunter. Headhunters are just one arrow in your quiver, but for many professionals this arrow will prove to be an important weapon in their battle to maximize their career opportunities.

As Ben has emphasized many times in *The Bigs*, you can't expect anyone, including headhunters, to do your work for you. The odds are, for most of your career moves, you will uncover the job opportunity through traditional networking—in other words, without the aid of a headhunter. Also, even if an interesting job opportunity is found by a headhunter, you shouldn't rely solely on the headhunter to sell you to the company as the best candidate. Be prepared to use your network to research the position independently, as well as to proactively use your network to help sell you as the best candidate for the job. Remember, the headhunter works for the company and he is typically reviewing more than 100 resumes per search and likely introducing 5 to 10 strong prospects to the company for the job you want. Always be respectful of the headhunter's position, but remember you can only depend on yourself to look after your best interests.

Finally, if you do what Ben tells you in *The Bigs*, and you become a stud executive in the health care industry (or you work at a PE firm that invests in health care companies), be sure to contact me—there is a good chance I can help. Best of luck to all of you!

Larry

TO B OR NOT TO B

I never got a master's of business administration degree, but without a doubt the degree makes sense for many young professionals. From talking to full-time MBA graduates, the consensus is the most value their MBA provided was the contacts they made in business school. Rarely will you find such a concentrated group of smart, interesting, and motivated people, and there is no telling what good things socially, intellectually, or professionally may come from those contacts.

MBA Financial Analysis

Despite the "soft" benefits an MBA may provide, for the majority of young professionals considering an MBA, the financial implications will be paramount. The question is, how do you measure this? While trying to peer into the future is always murky, here is a method to use as a starting point for your decision regarding the financial implications of an MBA. Let's treat your decision To B or Not To B as if it were a new business venture.

First, research the cost of the MBA programs you are considering. In this analysis, do not include the cost of room and board since if you decided Not To B you will still be paying for rent and food. If you are considering a full-time program, you do need to include the "cost" of earnings you will be foregoing for the two years you will be back in school.

Next, you must estimate the increase to your future earnings an MBA would provide. This is an imprecise exercise. However, all financial revenue projections for all new businesses are difficult to do and you need to give it your best efforts. Despite being imprecise, the process of constructing a financial estimate for the benefits of an MBA can be extremely valuable. It will make you think analytically about your career and research what financial value an MBA could provide you.

For example, let's say I've been working for three years at my first job out of college. Let's assume I had been doing well (this year I believe my total compensation will be $70,000), but I am considering getting a full-time MBA. After talking to as many people as possible about my planned post-MBA career path, I estimate getting an MBA will be worth an additional $30,000 in income to me per year, and that differential will likely last for an extended period of time. Now I am ready to put together a financial analysis. (Note: I multiplied all of my estimated forgone earnings, and increased future earnings, by .70 to account for my combined 30% federal and state income tax rate.)

Expenses

Tuition for 2 years	
($60,000 × 2)	$120,000
Foregone earnings for 2 years	
($70,000 × 2 × 0.70)	$98,000
Total expense	$218,000

Revenues

Estimated increase in annual earnings	
($30,000 increase per year × 0.70)	$21,000

Estimated Payback for Full-Time MBA

Total cost	$218,000
Divided by annual earnings increase	$21,000
MBA payback in years	10.4

This analysis shows that under my projected costs and income, the payback for my MBA would be 10.4 years. That is a pretty long time and if I only cared about the financial implications of an MBA, I probably would not do it. However, with *your* assumptions plugged in your payback might be much shorter.

While the above financial analysis is for a full-time MBA program, part-time MBAs have become increasingly popular. In fact, almost twice as many students attend part-time rather than full-time programs. For those of you thinking about getting an MBA, the decision to go full-time, or part-time, is of critical importance. Following are the pros and cons of both:

Full-Time MBA: The Pros

- Business school is a great way to reboot your career. If you want to change careers, or change companies, business school can be a big help in getting that accomplished. For instance, it might be difficult to switch into consulting if you have been teaching for a few years. If you can't get the consulting job you want, then consider going to business school and trying again in two years.

- For a small number of jobs, business school is virtually a requirement. For instance, if you want to be an investment banker, whose job it is to advise companies on strategy, having an MBA is often required. Also, for some consulting and corporate jobs, an MBA is considered important and occasionally is required.

- The contacts and friendships you make at business school can be valuable in your career. Generally, the more prestigious the business school the more valuable these contacts and friendships will be.

- You will be taught information that is useful in your career. While this is certainly true, the people I know who have gone through a full-time MBA program generally rank the information learned there as less important than the friend-ships, contacts, and increased career opportunities that went along with getting their degree.

Full-Time MBA: The Cons

- A full time MBA costs a great deal of money. In my previous analysis, it would cost $218,000 in after-tax dollars (at the assumed income tax rate of 30%, this is the equivalent of $311,000 of pre-tax earnings) to get a full-time MBA.

- You are spending two years not directly advancing your career in a specific industry or at a specific company.

Part-Time MBA: The Pros

- If you are getting your MBA part-time, it is likely you are also working full-time. Therefore, you are not foregoing your cur-rent compensation or your position in your company. Also, in some cases, your current employer may subsidize part of, or all of, the cost of tuition.

- Having an MBA may modestly change the perception of you within your current company. However, more significantly, having an MBA can make you more attractive to potential new employers if you decide to switch companies or industries. (That is one reason some companies have stopped subsidizing MBA programs for their employees.)

Part-Time MBA: The Cons

- Fairly or unfairly, a part-time MBA is often not considered to be quite as prestigious as a full-time degree; therefore, the power of a part-time MBA to reboot your career is somewhat diluted.

- The contacts and friendships one makes at a part-time program may be fewer and of less value than those made at a full-time program because the bonding that takes place in a full-time program is difficult to replicate in a part-time program.

- The time and energy spent studying for an MBA at night could be a drain on your personal and professional life.

Final Thoughts on To B or Not To B

At the end of the day, for both full-time and part-time MBA programs, the key driver for your decision To B or Not To B should be your career goals. If you are considering an MBA, you likely have been working for at least a few years and have a good idea of what you want your future to look like. With that knowledge, you need to network to find as many professionals as possible who have already accomplished your goals (or are on their way to accomplishing your goals). After these discussions, you need to come up with a plan of action and decide how business school, with its pros and cons, fits into that plan. If possible, it would be especially helpful for this mentor group to contain a mix of individuals who did, and did not, go to business school. Also, this network of senior professionals will be valuable to keep in contact with as you progress in your career. After you have done all that, you will be in a great position to decide the question of full-time, part-time, or no time.

Other Postgraduate Degrees

While this section only dealt with MBAs, many of you will consider getting other postgraduate degrees. Whether it be teaching, law, medicine, engineering, or any other discipline, the thought process and financial analysis is similar. Most importantly, the final step of the decision should be identical. Talk to as many professionals as possible who have been, or are now on, your prospective career path.

After these discussions, if you are still excited about your career plans and understand how a postgraduate degree fits in with these plans, you can pursue (or not pursue) your postgraduate degree with confidence—as well as a budding support network.

MATH, A GOOD COLLEGE, AND A HIGH GPA

I want to dispel the myth that it is important to be good at higher math to be successful in business. This is simply not true. What is important is to know how to add, subtract, multiply, and divide (which a $5 calculator can help you with). The important skill is learning which numbers you need to understand to manage your business. The most respected businessman of our era, Warren Buffett, commented succinctly on this issue when he said, "*The good thing about business is that you don't have to know any higher math.*"

To make the point, both Buffett and I oversimplify the case "against" higher math when we say it is unimportant in businesses. What we really mean is that it is unnecessary for the vast majority of jobs in business. However, for a small percentage of jobs (engineering, quantitative finance, and the like) it is a requirement. Accounting, though, is important for many jobs in business—especially jobs in senior management since it is the language of business. Even the ability to express yourself compellingly in writing is more important in business than higher math. So, if you are a student or graduate looking to take academic courses to strengthen your business skills, most of you should study accounting or English and forget about calculus or trigonometry.

With all that said, being good at math is certainly no handicap to success. Math is a form of logic and if you are able to translate that logic to business decisions you will have a valuable skill. However, in managing a business, always remember numbers are simply one tool to help you understand the quality of the job *people* are doing.

A Good College and a High GPA

If you attend (or graduated from) a good college, or have a high GPA, congratulations! Without question those achievements will make it easier for you to initially get a great job. However, *from your first day at work until the day you retire, no one will care where you went to undergraduate school, how you did there, or whether you have any graduate degrees.* They will care only about whether you are helping the company succeed, and if you don't you will be gone quicker than you can say "valedictorian" or "Ivy League." This reality should be encouraging for all students who attend less prestigious colleges and a warning to all who attend highly regarded ones.

Conversely, if you didn't go to a prestigious school, or have a high GPA, it may initially be more difficult to get a great job. However, it is absolutely doable and happens all the time. You may have to sell yourself harder, or start in a less desirable position, but many of the most successful people began just that way. *If you start a few rungs lower on the corporate ladder, and you do an outstanding job, my observation is it generally takes between one to three years for you to get on an equal footing with those who started above you. After that, it's game on!*

LIFE AIN'T FAIR

Life ain't fair in an infinite variety of ways, and since getting a great job is so important, this undertaking can rank right up there with some of the biggest "ain't fairs" you may encounter. For instance, I know a daughter of a friend of mine who walked into her first interview with no preparation and received a great job offer for a highly competitive position. Two years later, it took her brother, who was equally well-educated and presentable, more than 50 interviews to finally land a great job in the same industry.

It is likely some things in your life which should be difficult will turn out to be easy and vice versa. Things have a tendency to even out over time. If it happens your job search turns out to be one of the things which is very difficult, remember the old saying, "what doesn't kill you makes you stronger." Everyone I know who was subjected to a lengthy job search emerged from the experience smarter, tougher, and more determined to do a great job than when they began their search. *If your job search strengthens these three character traits, then a protracted job search could turn out to be the best thing that ever happened to you.*

THANK YOU NOTES

After getting your great job, it is important you write a thank you note to everyone you interviewed with. Not only is this a simple common courtesy, but it's very much in your self-interest. These were your best contacts during your job search and you may well end up working with, or for, some of these professionals in the future. *Also, it is likely your first job search will not be your last and you will probably need help from these individuals again in the future.* Following is an example of the type of email you should send:

Dear Mr. Jones,

I am writing to thank you again for speaking to me about my job search three months ago and to tell you my good news—I got a job! The name of the firm is First Co. and I will go through their training program and then be assigned to a department.

I want you to know how grateful I am for the time you spent with me. Your insights and advice were very helpful in getting me up to speed on the industry. I particularly liked your idea about (whatever), and I used it a number of times during my subsequent interviews. Without your help, and the help of a number of other Bowdoin College graduates, I am certain I would not have been ready to compete and get this great job opportunity.

Mr. Jones, below is my new contact information. I hope to see you soon, either professionally or perhaps at a Bowdoin College alumni event. Thank you again!

Sincerely,

Ben Carpenter

While most young people theoretically understand the importance of networking, very few will take the time to write a thoughtful note. You should write notes to everyone who helped you and make a concerted effort to stay in touch with individuals who could assist your career going forward. Everyone likes to hear good news, and everyone likes to be thanked, so use the happy occasion of getting a job to strengthen your network for the future.

YOUR STEP-BY-STEP GUIDE TO GETTING A GREAT JOB

STEP 1: Since your job search revolves around your contacts, start by documenting who these people are. On your computer or smartphone, organize your contacts into four categories: Family; Friends and Special Interests; CSO and Employed Students; and LinkedIn. For each contact be sure you have all the relevant contact information. When you first go through this exercise you may be discouraged by how few contacts you have. However, your network will grow dramatically over time as you successfully mine and leverage your initial contacts and your CSO.

STEP 2: Schedule a meeting with each of your initial network contacts to discuss where you are in your job search and to find out what (and most importantly who) they know that could be helpful to you. Don't assume they know you need help. This advice particularly applies to those closest to you: parents, siblings, and close friends. One of your goals during these initial discussions and informational interviews is to gain additional names to add to your network.

STEP 3: Once you have focused on an industry, and a job within that industry, you need to identify job openings. This can be done through your network by leveraging your informational interviews, searching employment websites, and being creative.

STEP 4: If a job lead comes through an employment website (or any source other than a contact within that company) you need to use your network to find a contact within the company who can get HR's attention focused on your resume. Hopefully, this will lead to you getting a job interview.

STEP 5: Once you have a job interview scheduled, again use your network to try to get at least one informational interview (in person or on the phone) with an employee at the company who is closely connected with the job you are seeking. *This allows you to display your preparation as well as tailor your sales pitch by knowing what skills and personal attributes the job requires.*

STEP 6: In addition to informational interviews, research the company online and conduct any other creative primary research you can think of. Also, before your interview, attempt to research your interviewer online or offline. Finally, prepare and practice punchy vignettes for the key points you want to make during your interviews.

STEP 7: You are now prepared to go into your informational and job interviews with excitement, determination, and the confidence which comes from being prepared. Keep a laser focus on how your talents, skills, and interests can help that company succeed. During informational interviews, remember to always "ask for the order" (i.e., ask if there are any job openings you can interview for). Also, remember to keep a call log and send follow-up emails (every month to your contacts in HR and every three months to your informational interview contacts) in order to "shake the trees."

STEP 8: Treat your job search like a game. Realize that for most people this game entails a good amount of rejection before they win and get a great job. Don't allow rejection to discourage you—use it as fuel for your determination.

STEP 9: After you get your great job, don't forget to write thank you emails to everyone you spoke to during your job search. Remember, it is likely you will need to use your network in your new job—or to get another job in the future.

Chapter 8

How to Do a Great Job

The genesis of this book was my eldest daughter, Avery, getting an offer for her dream job. In my panic to help her, I quickly jotted down some thoughts about how she could do a great job. My intention was to provide some basic information about the working world. However, after a few minutes, I realized I could not contain myself and my advice was more like tough love.

The next day when my longtime assistant, Lori, weighed in with her advice for Avery, I was shocked. Her advice was *much* tougher than mine. At that moment, I had an epiphany. While I worked closely with Lori for more than eight years and knew she was an incredibly competent professional, I had never paid close attention to her work methods. By reading Lori's advice to Avery, I came to appreciate how she approached her job and better understand how she is like the proverbial duck: calm and in total control on the outside, but paddling like crazy just below the surface to get everything done perfectly and make it all look easy!

While the advice Lori and I gave to Avery is a great foundation for all young employees, it is just that, a foundation. To build a great career you need to tailor your actions to the specific requirements of your job. The best way to understand how to do this is to closely observe how the top performers in your company get it done. *In any good-sized company or department there should be no need to reinvent the wheel. Imitate the actions of the star employees and then use your creativity and talents to perform even better.*

Some of the advice Lori and I gave Avery was specific to the job of being an executive assistant, but most of it applies to all jobs. Even the suggestions specific to Avery's first job are valuable for demonstrating the positive attitude and intense dedication you need to succeed. Below you will find Lori's and my notes to Avery reprinted in their original form. I left them this way because they have a raw, straight-from-the-heart, quality.

BEN'S ADVICE FOR AVERY

Set Your Sights High

- *Don't strive to do a good job; strive to do an outstanding job.* You are not going to be an assistant forever, but the impression you make on your boss could well have an impact on your entire career. This is an incredible opportunity, so make the most of it. You want your boss to believe you are the best assistant in the entire world.

- *Consistency of effort and actions are critical.* As a student, nobody expected you to be on your game 100% of the time. As a full-time employee, that *is* expected. If your effort or actions are subpar just 1% of the time, that 1% is all anyone will remember when they think about your job performance.

- *Meet all deadlines.* One basic requirement for doing an outstanding job is to handle all your work-related tasks, large or small, in a timely manner. If your job is to get a report done by Friday, get it done by Friday. If HR asks you to fill out a form today, do it promptly.

Your Boss

- *In this job you will be a gatekeeper*—granting or denying access to your boss. Everyone at work will know who you are and want you to help them in some way. Your primary job is to take care of your boss, but it is important everyone you come in contact with has a positive experience with you. In many companies, the most hated people are the boss's assistants who treat people in a high-handed way. Even if someone is a pest, rude, or stupid, always treat him respectfully. One day you may be working with, or for, that person. Also, bear in mind how your boss views you will be heavily influenced by what people in the company tell her.

- *Don't ever complain to anyone in the company about your job.* If it gets back to your boss she will think it unprofessional and wonder why you didn't talk to her directly. I hope the job will be awesome, but if it isn't you need to keep a positive attitude, do a great job, and at the earliest possible time get transferred into a job you want.

- *Assume everything your boss tells you is confidential.* You want to be a confidante of your boss, but that will only happen if she has total trust in your discretion. Also, realize the working world is identical to school in terms of keeping secrets. The only way to keep a secret is to not tell *anyone.* If you tell secrets to your friends, and rely on their good judgment and discretion not to say anything, you will often be disappointed. However, there is one difference between school and work. At school, a secret revealed could be embarrassing—at work it could cost you your job.

- *Always get to work earlier than your boss.*

- *Always stay later than your boss* unless she tells you to go home.

- *Initially do a lot more listening than talking.* If your boss wants to engage in a discussion of your ideas, or asks for your advice, then go for it. However, unless she specifically asks for your opinion, your focus should be solely on understanding what she wants you to do and then doing it…brilliantly! There will be a lot of time in the future to assert yourself and share your ideas.

- *Learn how to anticipate your boss's instructions.* Numerous times each day I tell Lori, "*Put this in my calendar*" or "*Get a copy of that report for me,*" and her response often is, "*I've already done it.*" The ability to anticipate instructions is one thing that defines a great employee.

- *If your boss takes you along to meetings* (fingers crossed) you should acknowledge this afterwards by saying, "*Thank you for including me, I learned a lot.*" You don't need to say this repeatedly, but if you acknowledge that she is going out of her way to help you learn, she will be more likely to keep inviting you.

- *You will need to ask a lot of questions* in order to do your job well. However, you should ask your boss questions only she can answer. For instance, "*Do you want to talk to Mr. X in person or by phone?*" But, if your boss tells you to go to Studio D to pick up a package don't ask her where that is—ask someone else.

Your Job

- *Quickly find one or more mentors or peers* who can answer your questions and show you the ropes. This step is very important for you to get up to speed.

- *If the person you are replacing is willing to help you,* pick his brain about how your boss wants the job to be done and get his phone number so you can call in the future with questions.

- *If you find you don't have the skills* to accomplish some piece of the job, such as creating spreadsheets or reports, don't try to fake it. Speak up immediately and find out how and where to learn the needed skill. Don't wait until it becomes a major problem.

When you start, your boss will not expect you to know every-thing, but in three months she will.

- *When you make mistakes* quickly own up to them. Apologize, correct the problem, and move on.

- *No task is beneath you* whether it's picking up dry cleaning, help-ing with children, or getting coffee. Whatever your boss needs to help make her day or life easier is part of your job.

- *Regularly ask yourself one question*: "If I was my boss, am I doing everything the way I would want it to be done?"

Other Important Issues

- *Never say anything negative about your co-workers.* Assume anything you say about anyone will get back to them. Follow this golden rule both inside and outside the company. You never know who might say what to whom and we all know it can be a *very* small world. Let others say bad things about people. You should stay above any negativity. Over time, people will respect you for this quality and see you as a true professional and leader.

- *Dating in the office is a bad idea.* It is unprofessional, distracting, and often leads to drama which is the *last* thing you or your boss needs to deal with. Also, if you date a co-worker, your boss will assume (correctly or incorrectly) that you share secrets about the office with your boyfriend and she will be less likely to trust you with sensitive company information.

- *This job is a great opportunity and the only way to do a great job is to feel rested and healthy.* You will need to get a reasonable amount of sleep and exercise regularly. There will be plenty of time to party on the weekends, but your top priority has to be your job.

- *Take your cue on how to dress from your boss.* You don't need to dress exactly like she does—just don't dress dramatically more or less conservatively. Keep in mind the old expression that you should "dress for the job you want, not for the job you have."

- *Don't be scared.* You are an incredible young woman and *more* than capable of doing this job exceptionally well. However, you will need to work hard, be disciplined, ask questions, and, most of all, pay attention!

LORI'S ADVICE FOR AVERY

Your Boss

- *Your #1 priority is making your boss look good.* Don't strive for recognition and credit; that will come naturally if you do your job well.

- *Confidentiality is key.* Your boss must be able to trust you with all aspects of her business and personal life. For example, don't share your boss's calendar with people without her permission. If your boss is golfing or getting a manicure, she is "out of the office." If she is in an interview, don't explain whom she is seeing. You want to be considered a vault, always error on the side of not sharing.

- *Treat anyone meeting with your boss with as much respect as you do your boss.* Whether it's a college student for whom your boss is doing an informational interview, or meeting with a board member, everyone wants to feel important and respected. If your boss is taking the time to see someone you should take the time to make him feel welcome and important. People, both inside and outside the company, will think it's a big deal you're arranging a meeting for them with your boss, so treat it as such. Don't be too casual even if your workplace is relaxed. The more professional you are, the more impressive your boss will seem.

- *Know whom your boss considers VIPs* and always treat them with respect, whether they are family, friends, or important business associates. Be professional but warm and greet these VIPs by name.

Work Habits

- *Aim to under-promise and over-deliver.* Work hard to help everyone meet deadlines, but be honest about what you can and can't accomplish in a given time frame. If your boss would like three things done by noon, and you may not be able to get it all done by then, be honest and say, "*I can get A and B done, but it might take me until 2:00 p.m. to do C. However, I will try my best to get all three done by noon.*"

- *Show up whether you're sick, you get a flat tire, there is a snowstorm, or you're hung over*—just show up. If you're truly ill, after a couple hours, ask to go home. Don't announce you're going home; ask if you can go home.

- *Schedule all personal appointments after business hours.* If your doctor doesn't offer late hours, find a new doctor. Do all personal errands on weekends. Don't go out to lunch or even run out to pick up a sandwich (unless that's the norm at your office). Be prepared to bring your lunch and eat at your desk every day.

- *Don't take any days off from work the first six months.* Don't take five or more consecutive days off during your first year. Despite your company's stated vacation policy, you really need to earn your vacation time. Bosses and co-workers get very unhappy when new employees are out of the office a lot.

- *Be available.* Always respond to emails and phone calls as soon as you can, whether late at night, early in the morning, weekends, or when you're on vacation. Anytime you receive an email from anyone at work with instructions for you to do something, be sure to respond immediately saying "*Got it*," or "*Will do*," or some similar acknowledgement you received the message. This makes life easier for the sender because they don't need to wonder if you received the message.

Office Dynamics

- *First impressions truly are everything*. Each time you meet someone you only have one chance to make a good first impression.

- *Treat all your peers with respect*. Build great relationships with other executive assistants. Offer to print things for their boss when he is visiting your office, arrange a car service, or order lunch. Respond to other executive assistants right away when they call or email about setting up a meeting. Establishing strong relationships with other EAs (inside and outside your company) will contribute to your success.

- *Don't let yourself get frazzled;* always remain calm and composed. If you're doing a lot of work, people know it and you don't need to draw attention to it. Don't have meltdowns when you're stressed. Take a deep breath and keep plugging away. If you make a mistake, or someone offends you, take a walk, get some air, do anything except burst into tears. You want people to perceive you as a mature business professional.

- *Don't overshare*: People don't care about your problem—they really don't. Everyone feels they have enough of their own and they didn't come to work to hear yours. When co-workers ask how you are, aside from your trusted work friends, the best answer is always "*Great, how are you?*"

- *Act like the job you have is your dream job*. Even if you know it's a stepping-stone to what you really want to do, don't mention that openly.

- *Don't complain about anything*: low pay, your cramped workspace, or any annoying co-workers. Don't be a squeaky wheel!

- *Be friendly and helpful to everyone you encounter*; it's good karma. One day you may need other peoples' help, and they will go above and beyond for you if you have done the same for them.

- *Don't talk about religion or politics at work;* you never know whom you might offend.

Chapter 9

How to Manage Your Finances

This last chapter is critically important because it is impossible to be a successful and happy entrepreneur, employee, spouse, or parent if you don't manage your finances responsibly. Looked at most simply, good financial management is nothing more than buying the right amount, of the right stuff, at the right time. Sounds easy enough, but most people (including yours truly) make many personal financial errors during their lives. While the consequences of mismanaging your finances are generally less early in your career, these consequences grow surprisingly quickly.

If you know very little about personal financial management you are not alone. Virtually no young adults understand the issue well. My favorite example is the daughter of a good friend who recently went through orientation with her trainee class at her first job out of college. A senior officer of the company spoke to the class and he, quite sternly, told the trainees he: "*expected them all to participate in the company's 401(k).*" Immediately after the class, my friend's daughter, quite distraught, called her father telling him, "*Dad, this is ridiculous. I'm not in good enough shape to do a 401k!*"

Regardless of how much you know right now, after going through this chapter you will understand the most important principles of personal financial management better than most seasoned professionals—even financial professionals.

KEEP YOUR PERSONAL EXPENSES LOW

For relatively successful people, there are two sides to achieving financial security: how much they make and how much they spend. Most people who have, or will soon have, a great job (like you!) spend too much time and effort worrying about how much they make and not enough time worrying about how much they spend. *Spending money will not make you happy and is like smoking cigarettes: Both are addictive and therefore much easier to start than stop.* While excessive spending is unlikely to kill you, if you take on debt to fund your spending habits, then just like smoking cigarettes, you will have done damage to yourself even after you kick the habit.

A recent survey of a large group of American adults asked how much money (income and net worth) they would need to feel comfortable financially. Interestingly, at virtually every level, the answer was *twice* their current income or net worth. On the surface, this sounds pretty surprising. Does someone making $30,000 a year (with a net worth of $75,000), and someone making $750,000 a year (with a net worth of $5,000,000), both feel that they need twice what they have? Upon reflection, however, the results of this study make perfect sense to me. That is because virtually *all* Americans, at *all* income and net worth levels, live beyond their means, and the sense of financial discomfort only grows as people get older and start thinking about retirement.

The easiest path to achieving financial security, or at least reducing financial stress, is to discipline your spending habits to lag your income. Specifically, if you don't yet make a lot of money, don't acquire a taste for expensive things like large apartments and fine wine. I promise you will be happier in a small apartment, drinking cheap wine, than you will be in a big apartment, drinking expensive wine, and having to worry about how to pay for it all.

Expenses are especially important to manage carefully because, unlike income, you are in total control. If you are an employee, your income is dependent on your boss. If you own your own company, your income is dependent on your customers. *Like everything else in life, put your greatest effort into managing what you control.*

Despite having a prudent financial plan, and the best of intentions to stick to it, you may occasionally spend more money than is consistent with your plan. This could be in order to buy a home, educate children, or any number of other legitimate reasons. Your plan is not meant to be a straitjacket, but if you stray it is important to get back on track with your plan as soon as possible.

A Dollar Spent Is Not a Dollar Earned

Benjamin Franklin quipped, "*A penny saved is a penny earned.*" Through the years and with inflation, that saying has morphed into, "*A dollar saved is a dollar earned.*" Earning and saving, however, are *not* equally important. Today, if you have a decent job, an additional dollar earned after federal income tax is only 64 cents, and after state and local income taxes it can be less than 50 cents. *Therefore, saving money is twice as important as earning money*!

KEEP IT SIMPLE, STUPID

I am a *huge* believer in the KISS principle, which is an acronym for "Keep it Simple, Stupid." The KISS principle can be applied to almost every aspect of your life (for instance, one love interest at a time generally seems to work best for all involved), but is particularly valuable in managing your financial affairs.

I first learned the KISS principle in my Banker's Trust commercial lending training program. Part of the program was a three-week intensive accounting course taught by a grizzled business veteran who had "seen it all" in the big leagues. While I knew I needed to learn accounting, what I really enjoyed was when Mr. Accounting gave us pearls of wisdom such as the KISS principle, and another nugget, the dangers of the word ASSUME. He told us to ever ASSUME anything we didn't know to be factual risked, "making an ass out of you and me." While I have done a pretty good job of following the KISS principle, I give myself much lower marks for ASSUME. I have often assumed things to be true, principally because I was in too much of a hurry to confirm them. "Think twice and act once" is good advice which, to this day, I have difficulty following.

INVESTING AND YOU

While there is much complaining that Wall Street is "rigged" against the average investor, I could not disagree more. In fact, I believe we are in a golden age for investing. I do agree individuals who attempt to actively trade the markets are at a significant disadvantage to "the pros," but this is the case in every walk of life. I would not want to play golf against Tiger Woods for money, so why should an amateur investor think he can out trade the Wall Street pros? Long-term investing, however, is completely different from trading. Today, indexed equity and bond mutual funds, or exchange traded funds, can provide diversified exposure to asset classes at less than 20% the cost of traditional mutual funds and less than 10% the cost of most hedge funds.

If you are not working in finance, or studying finance in school, the previous paragraph may sound like mumbo jumbo. In the spirit of KISS, let me simply tell you what to do. When you are ready to start investing, I recommend you call Vanguard, which is a mutual fund company that created the first indexed fund available to the public. There is overwhelming evidence to support the contention markets are efficient and money managers, as a whole, do not outperform by attempting to choose winning and losing investments. Indexed funds take the human element out of investing by simply owning a diversified basket of investments in a particular asset class. The largest index funds are those that track the Standard & Poor's 500 (which represents the 500 largest public companies in the United States).

Since index funds don't pay expensive money managers, and because they keep other expenses (including taxes) low by not actively trading, they are highly appropriate investment vehicles for individuals. If you buy and hold low cost index funds, you will benefit from the golden age of investing.*

I have an enormous, bordering on irrational, respect for America and Americans. One of the things I find especially attractive about Americans is their innate optimism. Optimism, however, is a dangerous personality trait to bring to your investment decisions. *As an investor, keep a healthy skepticism about everything you are told, and, especially, about everything you are sold.* Save your positive attitude and optimism for your interactions with your family, friends, and co-workers.

Happiness and Investing

The pleasure people feel from making a large amount of money is less than half as strong as the pain they feel from losing an equally large amount of money. I have no scientific evidence to back up

---

*If you save 1% a year on fees, the impact over the long term on your investment portfolio will be stunning. For instance, if you increase your returns from 5% annually to 6% annually, compounded over 40 years, you will end up with 46% more money in your account!

this hypothesis; it comes solely from years of observing friends, co-workers, and acquaintances, who have both made and lost significant amounts of money investing. I have never seen anyone experience prolonged bliss from making a large amount of money. However, I have seen people psychologically devastated, for extended periods of time, from losing large amounts of money. This is yet another powerful argument in favor of a conservative and diversified approach to investing.

I am a conservative investor, but that does not mean I don't take risks. Everyone who has cash is forced to take risks, even if you literally put your money under your mattress because "mattress investing" runs the risk—actually near certainty—of losing money due to inflation. Despite the fact inflation has been relatively "tame" over the past 20 years (the Consumer Price Index has averaged 2.55% annually), if you had put $100 under your mattress in 1993, it was worth only $61 in purchasing power in 2013. If that isn't scary enough, consider the following scenario. If I had been given a gift of $100 on my first birthday, and stuck it under my mattress, in 2013, due to the ravages of inflation it would only be able to buy me goods and services worth what $12.50 could have bought me in 1958!

While I want to avoid risk, I also don't want to have my money lose value. Therefore, I invest in a combination of stocks and bonds. Since stocks are generally considered to have higher risk and reward than bonds, the real question is how much to invest in stocks—and this is where happiness comes into play.

The old rule of thumb is you should invest in stocks the percentage of 100 minus your age, which for me would be 44%. That is not an unreasonable starting point, but what I actually do is invest enough in stocks so when the market goes down sharply, I am not unhappy because I don't feel overinvested, and when the market goes up sharply, I am not unhappy because I own enough that I feel

I am doing well. For me, right now, that percentage is 40% in stocks and the rest in cash and bonds.

Being happy with the amount of stocks I own is also important because I am not tempted by greed to buy stocks when they go up, or scared into selling stocks when they go down. Active amateur retail investors typically buy high (when things feel good) and sell low (when things feel bad). This is, at best, a recipe for underperformance and, at worst, a recipe for financial disaster. Study after study has shown this is exactly why individual retail investors who actively trade their portfolios typically do *much* worse than "buy and hold" investors.

Chasing Returns

A logical question at this point would be, "*Okay, you've convinced me I should not actively trade my personal account. But why do I need to settle for the relatively modest returns of indexed funds when I could give my money to an active money manager or hedge fund who has significantly outperformed in the past?*" The reason is not a secret. It is required to be stated in most all investment literature: *past performance is no guarantee of future results*. No truer words were ever written.

When you invest in a fund because of past performance you are doing what is called "chasing returns." I felt compelled to learn the inadvisability of chasing returns the hard way. My failures to accurately pick future winners are too numerous and boring to bother recounting. But I am far from alone. Understanding which funds outperform because their managers are smarter than the collective intelligence of the market, and which outperform because they are lucky, is beyond difficult.

The problem is one of large numbers. There are approximately 10,000 hedge funds and it is nearly impossible to know whether a fund outperformed its peers because of luck (which many in a sample of 10,000 will experience), or because of rare talent (which only a few will be blessed with). The problem of discerning luck from talent is so horribly difficult that even firms whose entire raison d'être is to analyze hedge fund performance, and funnel money to the "best" ones, get this wrong as often as right. These feeder firms are called "funds of funds." Because of the poor performance of so many funds of funds, the popularity of this class of funds has declined precipitously over the past five years. *If they can't do it—neither can you or I.*

FILE THIS ONE AWAY FOR THE FUTURE

If your career is in technology or finance, at some point you could find yourself owning a large amount of stock in the company you work for. In those two industries, it is common practice for a significant percentage of an individual's compensation (sometimes 50% or more) to be paid in stock which vests (meaning ownership actually transfers to you) over a period of years. Companies do this to conserve cash as well as to incentivize employees to stay at the company, work hard, and care about the success of the company. If you find yourself in the happy position of owning a large amount of stock in your company, what should you do? *In a word—sell.*

Huge chunks of many employees' net worth have been destroyed, particularly during the dot-com bust in the early 2000s and the financial crisis of 2008, because employees held onto stock in their company they could have, and should have, sold. Even if you believe strongly in the future prospects for your company, you can't afford to "double up" on your risk by having your compensation, and a large percentage of your savings, tied to the fortunes of the same company.

The way to decide on the appropriate amount of stock to hold in your company is whether, if you had been paid in cash, you would have gone out and bought that much stock. If the answer is no, then sell at the earliest possible opportunity. (My personal belief is any more than 5% of your investible assets in a single stock is too much.) Always remember, when a stock feels its best is also when it is most vulnerable to going down.

HELPING FAMILY AND FRIENDS FINANCIALLY

Helping people close to you in ways others can't, or won't, is one of the most important and emotionally rewarding things you can do. If you find yourself in this happy position, be sure to always provide financial help in the form of a gift *not* a loan. There is a significant likelihood that any money you lend to people will not be repaid. Then, not only do you not get your money back, you also damage your relationship with that friend or family member because you will resent them, and they will feel bad about having screwed you.

Most importantly, making all financial help in the form of gifts keeps your contributions "right sized." You will not find yourself parting with money you can't afford to lose because you have the mistaken belief it will be repaid. If you do find yourself in a situation where a friend or family member needs more money than you can provide in the form of a gift, you can only help that person if they have hard assets (such as a car, boat, or house) that you can take for collateral. In this situation you *must* involve an attorney to make certain the loan is executed and secured properly.

I came by this knowledge the hard way. After I had been at Greenwich Capital for a few years, and had started to make some pretty good money, a friend asked to borrow $200,000 to bridge a cash flow problem as he bought one house and sold another. Always willing to help a friend, I happily loaned him the money—even though $200,000 was a lot of cash and I could not afford to permanently part with that much money.

You can guess the rest. I didn't hear from My Friend for months after he told me he would repay the loan. Then I heard through other friends he had sold his house and I wondered what was going on. I tried to get in touch with My Friend, which was not easy, and when I finally reached him, he was full of excuses and promises. This went on for *a year* while I became more and more pessimistic about ever seeing my money again. Finally, I called my lawyer and he sent a letter to My Friend stating legal proceedings had been started against him. Thankfully, that got the desired result, but I vowed to *never* put myself in that position again.

A TIME AND A PLACE FOR EVERYTHING

Everything in this chapter about saving and investing is critically important for you to understand. However, during your first few years out of college, some things are even more important: going out, meeting new people, and having fun. This is true for several reasons:

- Your social friends and contacts can be important to you professionally.

- To live a happy life, you need a wide group of good friends to share it with.

- To live a happy life it is *very* helpful to have a spouse to share it with and you need to be "out there" (at places like the Tumble Inn!) to meet that person.

So, if for the first few years, after paying rent on your inexpensive apartment and drinking beer or cheap wine with your friends, you don't have much money saved—that's okay. There's a time and place for everything!

YOUR STEP-BY-STEP FINANCIAL PLAN

STEP 1: If you work for the rare company that still offers a 401(k) matching program, you *must* fund your 401(k) up to that matching amount (even if it means borrowing money to do it). A 401(k) match is the equivalent of an immediate 100% return on your investment. *That* is one opportunity which is *way too good* to pass up.

STEP 2: Keep your expenses as low as possible.

STEP 3: Pay off all credit card debt (and consider a debit card instead). The interest rate on credit card debt is normally in the high teens (recently averaging 17%). This is too high a rate for any business, or even any country, to pay without eventually going bankrupt—and you are no different.

STEP 4: Fully fund the *unmatched* portion of your 401(k). Funding your 401(k) is important because your money goes in pre- tax and compounds pre-tax. While you are young, most of your 401(k) savings should be invested in low cost indexed equity funds. The traditional rule of thumb for your equity allocation percentage is 100 minus your age.

STEP 5: Save six months to a year's worth of living expenses and invest these monies in a low risk, easily accessible, money market type fund. This money is to tide you over in case your income is interrupted because you leave your job, are fired, or your company goes out of business.

STEP 6: Pay down the principal on all your remaining debts, including mortgage debt, in order of most expensive first. Despite relatively low interest rates on mortgage debt, realize if you have *any* debt, and you also have an investment portfolio, it is as if you are borrowing money to make those investments. If you wouldn't do that, then you need to pay off all debt (which I believe is a good idea) before you become an investor.

STEP 7: Congratulations! You are now debt free, have started saving for your retirement with your IRA, and are ready to embark on additional savings. If you are not an investment professional, Vanguard's "Target Retirement" funds are a reasonable place to invest your money. These funds automatically rebalance your investment mix of stocks and bonds as you get older. It is the ultimate "buy and hold" investment vehicle for non-professional investors.

STEP 8: When you get to the stage where you have dependents (this could be parents or siblings, but more likely a spouse and then children) relying on your income to live, you need to buy life insurance on yourself. You should only buy term life insurance since it is the simplest form of life insurance. While you are young, term insurance is very inexpensive and well worth the cost to protect the ones you love.

Chapter 10

One Last Story

When a person looks back on his life, often a handful of random events have determined his fate. That has certainly been true for me: swearing at my baseball coach led me to Hotchkiss, Leigh putting her foot down about my nightclub plan led me to Greenwich Capital, and my aortic dissection led me to sales management. Nothing, however, has been more important for me than a single night at the beginning of my sophomore year of college.

I vividly remember the moment I first saw Leigh. It was the second day of school and the first night of Rush Week. My fraternity was in full swing, the music was cranking, and the energy was electric. Leigh was a freshman, tall, blonde, and tan. I saw her across the room talking to my best friend, John Small, whom I have often heard women describe as having "movie star good looks." Approaching beautiful women I didn't know had never been my forte, but seeing John talking to this girl gave me more courage than I usually possessed. I pushed through the crowd and made a beeline over to them.

At that point, I realized I had no plan. I knew I couldn't compete with John on looks, so I opted for aggression. I literally pushed him aside, introduced myself, and started talking a mile a minute about anything and everything I could think of to hopefully attract this girl to me. Leigh did seem a little amused, but not much more. At best, I think she gave me some credit for the obvious, if clumsy, effort I was making.

At the earliest possible moment I could claim to have established any kind of connection with her, I asked Leigh if she wanted to go over to the Chi Psi House where there was another party. I offered to take her into enemy territory because it was Rush Week and I knew that she would be interested in seeing other fraternities. (At Bowdoin, at that time, there were no sororities. Girls who wanted to join a Greek house joined fraternities and were designated "little sisters.") I was still worried she would say no…and I was thrilled when she said yes! I think she may have agreed because she hoped it would make me stop talking for a moment.

Stepping into a beautiful crisp Maine September evening, I could not believe my luck. Amazingly, it felt like I was actually making progress—but my worries were only starting. We walked into the party at Chi Psi and I immediately felt like a lone offensive lineman trying to prevent the Chi Psi boys from sacking my freshman quarterback. There were too many of them, I could not block them all, and a number of them got through with a clear shot at Leigh. Then the second amazing thing happened. While only a freshman, Leigh played the game with the poise of a senior, deftly eluding all the lunging tackles and staying on her feet.

After what seemed like an eternity, but was probably less than an hour, Leigh either tired of the game or took pity on me and, touching me for the first time, gently put her hand on my shoulder and asked if we could leave. Then, the *most* amazing moment of my life happened…when Leigh let me do something I will never forget…she let me walk her back to her dorm and, at the front door, allowed me to kiss her (once) good night before she disappeared. The entire way home to my apartment I was three feet off the ground—walking on air!

There is no official lesson here, just that fate sometimes smiles upon you and changes your life forever.

Letter from the Author

Dear Reader,

I hope this book has been helpful to you. I know I have given it everything I had to give. Finishing this challenging, and at times emotional, project is satisfying. However, I also feel a touch of melancholy because working on *The Bigs* has been so much fun, and I will miss it.

This book started out as my panicked advice for Avery and turned into something quite different. Most of the time, I haven't felt like a father talking to his daughter, or a teacher in front of his class. Rather, I have felt like an old man on a park bench telling a new friend what he learned during his life and career. Thank you for listening.

If you had the gumption to read this book, I know you can achieve your hopes and dreams. I'm rooting for you!

Your friend,

Benjer

Acknowledgments

TO MY MOTHER AND FATHER

I am dedicating this book to the memory of my father and to my mother. Together they raised five children, who now have 12 children of their own. Dad set an example for us by never giving up, never complaining, and always moving forward. Likewise, Mom showed us how to love, support, and fight to protect your family.

MY GIRLS

This book is about how people can best realize their dreams. The most important dream I have realized in my life is being blessed with my three daughters, Avery, Kendall, and Cameron. You all make me so proud and I love you beyond words.

MY SISTERS AND BROTHER

To my sisters, Lindsey, Helen, and Frances, and my brother, Arthur, for being the kind of siblings who love and support each other through life's journey.

MY EXECUTIVE ASSISTANTS

Lori Beaton has been a joy to work with every day since we met eight
years ago—thank you! Additional thanks to Lori for suggesting I
write this book and the huge contribution she made to *The Bigs* (and
to Avery!) with her "How to Do a Great Job" advice. Lori's deskmate
and partner at CRT, Valerie Cavallaro, has also been critical to the
success of this project, and I greatly appreciate her unstinting support and hard work. Thank you both for rolling with the punches
on this crazy, out of the blue undertaking, for being my sounding
boards, and for making the process of creating *The Bigs* so much fun.

MY FRIENDS

To John Nussbaum, for his strong encouragement to write my
stories, and my niece, Liz Toomey, and her friend, Siri Uotila, for
their advice on how to structure and organize those stories. To
Nancy Better, whose passion and expertise were instrumental in
helping *The Bigs* achieve its potential, and to my agent, Beth Davey,
for her invaluable advice that, "It's all about *your* heart and *the* read."

MY BOSSES, PARTNERS, AND DOCTORS

Thanks go to Ted Knetzger and Bill Rainer (for starting Greenwich
Capital—the firm where my dreams came true for 22 years), Gary
Holloway (my boss for many years at Greenwich), Jay Levine
(my partner at Greenwich and now CRT), and Doug Marzonie
(my sales partner at Greenwich for many years).

I also want to thank Aquiline Capital Partners, the private
equity firm that is the lead sponsor of CRT Capital. Without Jeffrey
Greenberg, Steven Spiegel, and Geoff Kalish believing in us, CRT
would look nothing like it does today. These guys are smart, tough,

and honest; in other words, great partners. It has been an honor (and a lot of fun!) to work with you all. It has been quite a ride and, happily, it is not over yet.

Last, but not least, my doctors—Chris Edelman, Mary Roman, and Len Girardi—deserve tremendous thanks for your world-class professionalism, expertise, and friendship, and for keeping me of this world.

MY WIFE, LEIGH

You saved my bar, my career, and my life. If that weren't enough, you have given me three beautiful daughters, and made the past 35 years feel like a dream I don't ever want to wake up from. You are the love of my life—thank you, thank you, thank you!

Index